A Whole Lot More Like Me

Loving My Comfort Zone

George E. Willock

Copyright © 2018 George E. Willock

All rights reserved.

ISBN 9781724282330

Dedication

The Network Marketing Sales Model (NMSM) provides one of the most, if not the most equitable and fair method of compensating people in the Free Market System. However, the majority of the training within the NMSM in both personal growth and financial independence is driven by a philosophy, mind-set, and tools which do not provide a platform for the majority of people to achieve success. The information contained in this book is made available to offer concepts, tools, and systems so that a greater number of people will have access to the means to attain the success they envision in the NMSM.

Additionally, through the use of this information, readers who apply these concepts, tools, and systems will be able to serve others, helping others also to achieve the success they envision for themselves. This book is dedicated to a non-Network Marketing concept, mind-set, and tools to inspire, encourage, serve, uplift, and challenge people to become what they were designed, created, and destined to be. This book is for those who value the freedom and independence that the Network Marketing Sales Model provides in personal growth and financial independence and who are willing to make a paradigm shift which will change their mindset to prove that there is a non-Network Marketing approach to success in the Network Marketing Industry.

CONTENTS

	Acknowledgments	vii
	Introduction	1
1	dōTERRA®, A Non-Multilevel Marketing Movement of People	21
2	Movements	35
3	Building a Movement	45
4	Perpetuating the Movement	53
5	Principles of Multiplication	69
6	Relationships: Foundations of Success	77
7	The Genius of You...Talents and Strengths	105
8	Sharing – Consultative Sales	131
9	Consultative Sales – Helping Others	139

CONTENTS

10	The Consultative Sales Process Stage 1 – Product Knowledge	145
11	The Consultative Sales Process Stage 2 – Prospects	155
12	The Consultative Sales Process Stage 3 – Getting the Appointment	163
13	The Consultative Sales Process Stage 4 -Initial Meeting/Assessing the Needs	167
14	The Consultative Sales Process Stage 5 – Presenting the Solution(s)	173
15	The Consultative Sales Process Stage 6 – The Close	177
16	The Consultative Sales Process Stage 7 – Follow Up or Teammate Education	185
17	Conclusion – More Like Me	189

Acknowledgements

To Norma:

For without her belief in me and her willingness to work out our philosophy so that others may excel to greatness, there wouldn't be this handbook of leadership.

For the unknown hours of pouring her life into the lives of those on Team Willock as well as those who are on other teams in order to better serve and lead people on their journeys to becoming who they were created to be, unique and authentic.

To Team Willock:

For their willingness to listen to our alternative ideas on building a business through Non-Network Marketing concepts and tools in order to utilize what we believe are better ways of loving, serving, and leading people. For their courage to not only listen to and act on the concepts, systems, and processes which provide the "how to" of making their "why" become reality.

To Team AromaSoul and their charismatic and dynamic leader,

Kalli Kenney:

As she has graciously allowed me to work with her team leaders, her team, and for her pursuit of leading others so they may become and experience God's wonderful plan for their lives.

Introduction

Dr. David K. Hill, Chief Medical Officer at dōTERRA®, said at their international convention in 2015 that, "we are a non-MLM company in an MLM industry." That statement caught my attention! It so captured my attention that I asked others who were in attendance what they thought of Dr. Hill's statement. Sadly, when asked, most people didn't even remember his saying it and those who did remember didn't have any idea what he meant. So, the question is, "what was Dr. Hill alluding to in his statement?" Let me share with you what my first thought was when I heard this revolutionary statement and what I think he meant.

My first thought was, "what would the necessary elements for success be in building a business and a team within a non-multi-level marketing company which is in a multi-level marketing industry?"

This chapter is what I think he meant by his statement and my process in arriving at this thinking.

This dichotomy of being a non-MLM company in a MLM industry has been the foremost business question on my mind for the past several years. And now I'm ready to reveal my findings in offering my answers to this all-important question.

First, there has to be a willingness to have or be in pursuit of a change in a person's mindset. There has to be a paradigm shift in our thinking. This paradigm shift begins with valuing people more than things. It's placing people at the center of getting things, work, done. There is a lot of lip service given to this by people in their

> *"Success is getting people done through work!"*

hope that by singing the right words of "people first, work second," they will entice enough people to believe and follow. That is until the other people find out that these singers are all show and no go. But, when there is a true shift in both our thinking and in our doing, we begin the adventure of living our unique and authentic lives. Then, when people do follow us, camp on our front steps to learn, and inspect us to see if we're the real deal, we're found worthy as leaders. We are found to be real, authentic.

We begin by changing our mindsets and we prove our mindsets worthy by using tools which align with this change in our thinking and acting. I've found there are four conceptual areas of growth for our becoming and being unique and authentic in a non-MLM. One of these conceptual areas requires a shift in our mindset paradigm while the other three require unique tools in addition to this shift. The first, which doesn't require special tools is knowing, understanding, and implementing what is known as a movement. The other three concepts require unique tools which are designed for people to learn of their uniqueness and then be able to apply their uniqueness for the benefit of others. These three are first building positive relationships, knowing our talents and strengths, and using a consultative approach to introducing others to our concepts and products.

I've devoted a chapter to each of these concepts and tools. Within each chapter, we'll go a little deeper into what and how these concepts and tools are vital to a person's success. However, please don't think I've exhausted or plumbed the depths of these concepts and tools within this book. We'll explore these four concepts and tools here, keeping in mind there is more, much more, to learn and apply. We just want to get headed in the right direction with this work. So, here we go!

To build a successful team with dōTERRA® as your science company and wholesale provider of essential oils, you must first know and believe that your business is a relationship building business. I've coached Wellness Advocates and Wholesale Customers across several teams having explained and worked with them on these concepts and tools. In doing this, there arises a puzzling question which many have voiced regarding my own style of behavior and my own talents and strengths. The question is actually an assumption. I have a unique ability in that when I'm coaching people through their strengths, the relationship that is formed appears to them to be based on my having relationship building strengths, which have been honed, in building relationships. Unfortunately, I don't have natural talents and strengths in the area of relationship building. In fact, out of a possible 34 strengths as identified by the Gallup organization, I don't have any relationship building strengths in my Top 10 Strengths. My first relationship building strength is in my 11th position out of 34 strengths. Additionally, as a certified SOCIAL STYLE® and Versatility Instructor, I am often perceived by people that my behavioral style is similar to their own. However, very few have seen me as having the style I was born with, the Driving Style. What others have seen is a high versatility of my behavioral style and a skilled application of my using my talents and strengths. As I coach individuals, I have a Driving Style demonstrating Relationship Building capabilities using non-Relationship Building talents and strengths. This didn't come about or happen overnight. It has been a long journey for me and the journey isn't over yet! But, the early-in-my-life paradigm shift in my mindset, and the learned and practiced skills provided through the implementing of the tools and concepts discussed in this book are a result of what I wrote on a 3x5 note card just prior to my graduating from college. What I wrote was a single sentence, but it was what drove me then and it drives me to this day. But, before I tell you what it is, I'd like to lay some groundwork of who I was and the milestones of change which took place during this journey.

The Start

In the early years of my life, accomplishing goals and pushing toward my objectives were more important to me than the growth and nurturing of others. For me, it was important to set a goal, determine what the steps would be for me to accomplish that goal, and then utilize anything and anyone to help me achieve my objective. Being focused on achieving results was as natural for me as breathing, and I thrived on it.

As a freshman in college, I was studying for a degree in English so I took classes which focused on various authors and their writings. One of those authors who was (at that time) also one of my heroes was Henry David Thoreau. In my reading assignments for that class, I learned that Thoreau had built a cabin with his own hands near a pond in a woods. This intrigued me. I thought it would be great for me to build my own cabin, write poetry and prose, hunt when I'd like, and fish when I'd like. This to me was the best life could offer and I figured it was exactly what I wanted. When asked what I was planning to do with my life, my response was that I was going to be a writer, live on the shore of a pond or a lake with a woods, and write what I wanted. I was 18 years old.

Shortly after deciding on how I would spend my life, I became a Christian, and I started on a very different journey which has forever changed my life. The milestones on this journey have marked some interesting twists, turns, roadblocks, and outcomes, but the foundation of knowing my Christ has always been my mainstay, my bottom line, through which all of my decisions ultimately have been filtered and upon which my decisions have been made. To better explain my journey, I'll be using the concept of milestones as markers on this journey that have radically impacted my life and how they have changed my perspective and behavior in developing relationships with others and the building of people.

Milestone 1

In 1976, I was sitting at my desk in the garage I had converted into an office. I had been in Fort Collins, Colorado attending meetings, seminars, and convocations for the annual staff training with Campus Crusade for Christ (Cru). While I was at staff training I purchased some cassette tapes, one of which was by a speaker who had been a recurring presenter at previous staff trainings that I'd attended. The speaker, Dr. Howard Hendricks, a professor at Dallas Theological Seminary, was teaching on leadership and discipleship using Jesus as the example for us to become leaders and disciplers of others. It was while I was in my office, listening to the tape by Dr. Hendricks when I heard him say, **"if there is anything that turns you on more than people, then you are wrong, because people always turned the Master on!"** This stunned me. The thing that turned me on more than anything else was fishing. For years, I'd been making jokes about finding a way to have a ministry to the fish; you know, sharing with the fish how they could have a meaningful, fruitful, and abundant life; how they could improve the quality of their life through a personal relationship with Christ. Quit sneering! It may have been tongue-in-cheek at the time, but there is a lot revealed in this statement regarding my thinking and acting as regards interacting with people at that time. While I was still in college, I went so far as to ask a mentor of mine how I could find Scripture verses that would justify my spending time fishing.

> *"if there is anything that turns you on more than people, then you are wrong because people always turned the Master on!"*

But, what I heard on Hendricks' tape on that day stopped me in my tracks. I knew for the first time that if I wanted to become more like Christ, if I wanted to be a discipler, if I wanted to become a leader, I would have to change. And, I would have to change significantly in both my thoughts and my actions. I knew I needed to become more mature in my thinking. To me this meant a change in my mind-set which would lead to a more mature demonstration of my actions. This became a pivotal point in my thinking. I must change. I must grow into being the person others are willing to follow. Yes, me.

A few years earlier, at a Campus Crusade for Christ annual staff training conference, Dr. Bob Smith, a retired pastor and college professor, defined "maturity." In Dr. Bob's message, he quoted a psychologist by the name of Gordon Allport, PhD. Allport was a leading psychologist who focused on the healthy personality of people rather than the neurotic or unhealthy person. In doing this, he created a criteria list of what a healthy person is, which included a definition of a mature or maturing person. Maturity as Allport defined it is the "integrating force of personality which orients behavior toward those events that make

> Maturity is the *"integrating force of personality which orients behavior toward those events that make long-range, lifetime, self-determining goals come true"* Gordon Allport
>
> *In other words, the more my actions reflect and align with my philosophy of life, then I grow in my maturity, but first I must know what my philosophy of life is; everyone has one, most have never identified it as such.*

long-range, lifetime, self-determining goals come true." It is this definition which Dr. Bob used that day when addressing the staff of Cru.

However, I knew that for my actions to follow my thinking, that is for me to change in action and not just in thinking, I needed more time to ponder what this meant. I'd established my life's goal (today it's called my 'why') as a college senior, nearing graduation. With Hendricks' unintended challenge, I had to decide if what I'd written out on a 3x5 notecard was what would drive me and cause me to stay the course over my life or was if it just a fun idea whose time had come and gone. I knew I had to either recommit to my new found thinking (a paradigm shift) and be willing to continually change for the duration of my life, or I had to walk away from what I was doing as a discipler and leader. In order for me to make an informed decision, I chose to study the Bible passage which Dr. Hendricks used in his seminar on tape. I turned to John 21 and began to read an already familiar passage, but this time it was in consideration of a fork in the path of my journey toward walking with Christ.

Jesus was speaking to Peter, asking Peter if he loved Jesus. The question was asked three times by Jesus toward Peter as to whether Peter loved Jesus. For the first two responses, Peter used a different definition of love from what Jesus was asking. The third time Jesus asked Peter, it was using the same definition of love that Peter had responded with the prior two times. For each of the responses Jesus told Peter to tend his lambs, feed his sheep, and tend his sheep. However, what struck me that day was not which definition of love Jesus used when asking Peter if he loved Jesus and it wasn't whether it was to tend or feed Jesus' sheep. No, what struck me was that Jesus never asked Peter if he liked sheep. Peter was a fisherman. Jesus was asking Peter to change his profession from being a fisherman to being a shepherd. For the first time in my life I had to admit that I really didn't want to be a shepherd, I wanted to be a fisherman. If the most important "thing" in this world to Jesus was people and I wanted to be a discipler, a leader, and more like Jesus, then I needed to have people become the most important "thing" in my life. I just had to get over one tiny little hurdle. I didn't like sheep! Sheep tended to get in the way of my objectives.

Henry Ford, the founder of The Ford Motor Company, once said, "When I ask for a pair of hands to work on my assembly line it seems they always come with a brain attached." Whether Henry was talking about the creativity of a person or whether his need for a pair of hands meant that he didn't want all of the complexities of personality and the other elements of a person attached to the pair of hands, the difficulty was that Henry just wanted someone to get the work done. And boy, how I could relate to this!

To me, sheep were the people who constantly got in my way of getting things done. All I really wanted to do was achieve the things that I believed were of value to me and, on a loftier plane, what I believed were of value to the kingdom of God: reaching people for Christ. Hopefully, when you read this you're not either eating or drinking and choking on what I just said. The inconsistency, the incongruency, of what I just said never dawned on me, not for a second. And in reality, I probably was just about like almost everyone else is in their thinking, if they're going to be honest with themselves: that people can be the biggest nuisance, the most inconsiderate, obstinate, and unthankful critters in the entire world. No wonder Jesus compared us to sheep! Yet, here I was debating within myself and with God on the value of what Dr. Hendricks had just stated.

As I said earlier, it was on that day, in a garage converted into an office, that I started down a path that would ultimately change me, and from which I would never recover. I say it was a path because my change didn't happen overnight, nor did it occur in the next weeks or months. It was to be walked out over time. As a matter of fact, it was years later when there had been adequate problems and obstacles placed in my path for me to overcome, which was my testing ground, that I was ready to start down the next segment of the path in this journey.

Milestone 2

For the next six years I thought about and worked through various situations. I was learning how valuable people are to God and yet, how I often failed still having such a long way to go. In 1982, I was seated in a comfortable, overstuffed chair in a psychologist's office where he had just finished asking me a question. But before those of you who know me begin to nod your head in confirmation of my need to see a psychologist, I'll share with you my purpose for sitting in that psychologist's office. I had been promoted to a higher level of sales management and the company for which I worked required everyone who was making a management positional move to meet with the company's psychologist in order to determine if we'd have difficulty in our new duties. So, even though some of you who know me may have thought that it was completely understandable that I should be examined by a psychologist and that I probably escaped too soon from his care, let me assure you that in this instance that wasn't the case.

Sitting in that overstuffed, very comfortable chair, I waited as the psychologist looking at me said, "George, you look uncomfortable. Why don't you take your suit coat off and throw it in that chair beside you?"

Right, I know, what kind of a question was that to ask of me when my purpose in being in his office was to get on with the interview, so I could get back to my family. After all, once I left his office, my family and I had to drive 2 hours to my sister's house with another 2-hour drive from her house to home. It was just before Christmas and there was a lot more for me to get done for the family in order for us to celebrate. My response to him was, "Why would I want to do that?" But it was his response to my answer that took me completely by surprise.

He said, "This is exactly what we need to talk about today. There is no doubt that you are driven to achieve and that you have been successful in your career. You were just here about a year ago and already the company wants you in a higher management position. However, here is the problem. You're not approachable by others to help them become more effective in their lives and that is what this job will be requiring of you - to be able to connect with others in order to help them become successful."

For the next two hours we talked back and forth, and quite frankly, I couldn't tell you anything at all about our topics of discussion. All I could remember then and now is that I needed to change, that I was not open, friendly, and easily approached by others. This was a crushing blow to me because I thought I had worked so hard toward becoming more like Christ in loving people only to find out I still had a long way to go. Had I made some strides toward my goal of caring for others? Yes, but I had not arrived. The psychologist was a credit to his profession and a terrific adviser to me in helping me to understand my need to grow in the area of loving people. However, I realized in talking with him that I had not yet become the person I needed to be in order to better serve others and help them become who they were created to be. For the first time in my life I was beginning to see that this would be a continuing process at every level of my personal growth.

Traveling home, my family and I stopped at my sister's house which was approximately halfway between Minneapolis and our house in Moorhead, MN. While at my sister's, I opened up and began to share with her what had transpired between the psychologist and me. Before I could get out more than letting her know that I had just come from meeting with the company psychologist, she blurted out, "What, are you nuts?!" I assured her that I wasn't any more "nuts" than normal, at least, what was normal for me. I then continued my recounting the discussion between the psychologist and me. When I was finished, my sister looked at me and smiling said, "He's right. All our lives whenever we'd ask you questions, most of the time you'd barely answer with anything other than 'yes,' 'no,' or at best a brief sentence. Even when you would come home from college you'd barely give us any answers." My response to her was, "Wow! Whenever you asked me any questions, I thought I was saying too much and would keep trying to shorten my answers." This was the first time I, without effort, became aware of myself through the eyes of another person and realized that the person I thought I was and who I showed myself to others to be weren't the same person. I needed to find the real, public and private, me.

Milestone 3 – Relationship Building Tool

A couple of years after my eye opening discussions with the psychologist and my sister took place, I was asked to become part of our company's training team. The team consisted of the manager, our coordinator, and me. Our job was to train the company's field agents on how to become more effective in their selling process. The strategy employed was to use field seminars, joint field and office work with the trainers of the agencies, home office seminars, and week-long education and training courses. In the week-long education and training courses we invited between 25-30 agents at a time in a company with about 600 agents to come to the company's headquarters. We'd start at 8 am and ran the courses until 9 pm with breaks for lunch and dinner. During this week, as part of the curriculum, the first day was spent on the introduction, education, training, and role-playing in the area of relationship building. The tool we used is called SOCIAL STYLE®. SOCIAL STYLE® is a behavioral style model used to help people build relationships with others. It provides a platform to improve our interpersonal skills development.

This behavioral style model is based on years of research of people in the workplace. This research showed that people exhibit one of four styles of behavior, each with their own preferred way of acting, thinking, and making decisions. By understanding these preferences, the agents could identify their own style of behavior and determine the best way to interact with both their prospect's and their client's preferred styles of behavior. I had gone through a half-day seminar on this material a couple of years earlier and had seen its value in my life and in my working with others. However, now I was going to be able to get some in-depth training and would then train others on this model of building relationships.

This model was so beneficial and influential, not just to me but to those agents who applied it when building relationships with others, that our manager even went so far as to state, "This program has updated and replaced the old Golden Rule philosophy and the old way of thinking. Now we've got the 'Platinum Rule'!" And for a long time all of us believed he was right...until I found out what the Golden Rule really teaches.

As a boy, living on a small farm, near a small town, I attended (rarely) Sunday School classes in church and I learned about the Golden Rule. "Do unto others as you would have them do unto you." The way I understood what this meant was that if others would do for me what I really wanted them to do, this old world would be a much better place - at least for me. Little did I realize then or for many years that this was one of the most misunderstood verses in the Scriptures. This wasn't talking about my treating people as I'd like to be treated. No, it was talking about my finding out how others preferred to be treated, then going out of my way to treat them that way. I needed to first know about them before I could relate to or help them.

Once I took the time to study and learn what the Golden Rule teaches, I realized there has been and continues to be a significant amount of faulty thinking by many parties. There are those who wish to continue to believe in the Golden Rule but continue to incorrectly teach what Jesus meant. They find comfort and solace in staying true to their beliefs. For their staying true to what they believe, I applaud them. However, by continuing to misunderstand and to teach what the Golden Rule was never meant to teach or how it should be applied is doing a disservice to both those who also believe in the words, wisdom, and life-changing impact of Jesus and to those who don't.

Then there are those who have maintained a superficial knowledge and comprehension of the Golden Rule, creating a "strawman" argument or position in order to promote their program(s), product(s), or philosophy(ies).

They loudly proclaim their having found a way to replace that old-fashioned, inadequate, and deficient cliché called the Golden Rule. They have found or in some cases (according to their literature) created the Platinum Rule and it jumps a person in understanding and working with others past the Golden Rule as fast as hyperspace in Star Wars is or warp speed in Star Trek.

> **Platinum Rule**
>
> *"...do unto others as they would want done to them"*
>
> Too many people to name take credit for this

The Golden Rule has always been about understanding the other person, knowing them, and identifying how they prefer to be treated, worked with, and cared for before we focused on how we preferred to be treated. Additionally, the Golden Rule has the caveat that we are to know how we prefer to be treated as well in order to be of service to others. *For additional insight into the Golden Rule vs. the Platinum Rule see the insert. (pgs. 96-98)*

> **Golden Rule**
>
> *"...do unto others as you would have others do unto you."* Matthew 7:12

Teaching and training on this relationship building model gave me the needed and appreciated grounding on how to be more effective in building relationships with others. SOCIAL STYLE® behavioral modeling was and is still a vastly important tool for me.

After working in our home office for just over one year, I was offered an opportunity to join the leading agency of our company as a Unit Manager. A Unit Manager position is a second line management position designed to provide training and experience before moving into an Agency Management position. My commitment to the home office was for a two-year stint as the Trainer for the company, but because the Agency Manager who offered me the position was also the most successful Agency Manager in the company, and he wanted me as soon as possible, I was released from this 2-year commitment at the end of 18 months to move to Omaha, Nebraska as a Unit Manager. That move for me was more than just my moving back into the field. That move led me to a key tool in valuing and helping people, and that key tool was equal to the value of what the behavioral model did for me.

Milestone 4 – Building on People's Strengths

While working at the Omaha Unit Office, I was invited by my Agency Manager to attend a daylong seminar in Lincoln, Nebraska on managing and leading others. One of the speakers at this meeting was Dr. Donald Clifton, a leading psychologist at the University of Nebraska Lincoln. Dr. Clifton spoke on the value of relationships and people, and he introduced a new concept to all of us. This new concept he spoke on was in reference to changing the way we think about people. Dr. Clifton explained that since shortly after World War I, psychology had taken a path of identifying what was wrong with people and trying to fix it. His approach differed from the norm in this path. His approach was to find out what is right with people, building on the things they are doing right; he called those right things "talent." He said everyone has talent, and he asserted that when a person combines his unique talents through their application those talents become strengths, and that by building on the strengths of people we can make the weaknesses virtually irrelevant. I had never heard of this before. Up until this time, both in my personal life and in my training of others in business, I operated by identifying the problem or obstacle and fixing it, going through it, around it, over it, or under it; but the focus was on fixing the problem. Everything I thought about and put into practice was spotlighting what was wrong and fixing it.

Now, I was listening to a person who seemed to know what he was talking about, who had the credentials to back up what he was presenting, and who had seen positive results from focusing on helping people develop their talents and strengths. It was as if a key had been inserted into a lock and suddenly what had been closed was now open and this sunshine of a new paradigm came flooding into my thoughts. Thinking to myself, I decided to take this approach. It was consistent with what I had toyed with in a number of other areas of my work and personal life. It just made sense. This began a new path on my journey of valuing people more than things and I knew that here was a tool that fit that value perfectly. I then began choosing to look for what people do right, identify it with them, and then help them build on that talent.

Why this Book?

My goal in the writing of this book is to offer a different approach, a different way of thinking, a different set of tools - a new paradigm, if you will, to our interacting with others. It is my hope that this book will help others learn that people are truly unique, valuable, indescribably more interesting than any fishing story, sporting event, business challenge, or single-minded venture we can ever imagine. It is my hope that we, that is you and I, discover that we have far more to give than we have ever believed we are capable of giving. It is my hope that when you read about the models and concepts along with the thoughts within this book, you'll come away with a belief that you truly were created to become more than you ever considered possible. I hope you will know that you truly were created uniquely and wonderfully, and that you were given great gifts from which you can provide benefit and service to others. And the greatest benefit to you? The greatest benefit to you is that you'll discover it is only in the giving away of these gifts for the benefit of others that you will be the one receiving the greatest benefits.

What did I write on that 3x5 notecard?

My goal is to live long enough to disciple (coach and mentor) the children, the grandchildren, and the great grandchildren of my generation.

1
dōTERRA®
A Non-Multilevel Marketing Movement of People

Personal disclaimer: The intention of this chapter is to provide the readers with assurance about how very unique and pioneering dōTERRA® is in the balancing of a for-profit venture with a nonprofit process. To accomplish this task is extremely demanding of those in dōTERRA®'s corporate leadership. It is not my intent to criticize or in any way denigrate the work begun and continuing to be done to help change this world's health and wellness through dōTERRA®'s corporate leadership or the Wellness Advocates so committed. However, due to my having successfully worked with movements, both in leading and directing, worked in professional sales, and my having studied and applied tools which bring out the unique and authentic talents of others, I'm offering for the reader's consideration thoughts, concepts, and processes that may not always perfectly align with what we see from mainstream corporate or field leaders. It is my hope these thoughts and processes will be of help to those of us who are Wellness Advocate builders and will be food for thought by the corporate founders of dōTERRA® as they continue to fine tune this balancing of for-profit and nonprofit venture.

I attended the 2013 dōTERRA® national convention not sure what to expect, other than the unbridled enthusiasm of my wife, Norma along with many others who attended. She had attended the 2012 national convention and came home bubbling over with enthusiasm, vision, and a new direction for her life. I was not unenthused, nor was I skeptical in my attending yet another convention. However, I do have to admit that after attending so many conventions and conferences in my business career, I wasn't looking forward to having to sit through three days of whatever was on the agenda.

As we were sitting, waiting for the convention to start, Norma kept looking at me for any telltale signs of my making a quick exit. Please don't misunderstand me at this point. My looking for an exit had nothing to do with dōTERRA®, but it had everything to do with sitting through meetings. However, very shortly the convention started with silhouettes of dancers spelling out themes of this convention. It took me a while to catch on to what they were doing. Artistic forms of most anything, especially of dance, is not a strength for me. But then, Norma leaned over and said, "isn't this just beautiful! They're spelling out in the silhouettes of their bodies various themes of the convention." At that moment, I caught on and began to appreciate what they were doing. I am very quick when the obvious is explained!

After this opening, David Stirling was introduced as one of the founders and CEO of dōTERRA®. Stirling made a few opening remarks about how excited he was to have so many people in attendance, that dōTERRA® was then in their 5th year, and that year's attendance was more than double from the previous year's attendance; a good sign of dōTERRA®'s growth. And then he began his presentation. Within a few sentences of his opening remarks he stated that if he had his way he would never build an organization but would create a movement. Immediately I was tuned in. For someone in the business sector to open their presentation with the concept of wanting to start a movement rather than an organization was unprecedented. I had been involved in a movement years earlier, in fact led a movement in one place and directed a movement in another, and ever since had spent time studying, thinking, and looking for signs of other movements. I found precious few.

> *Movement, not an organization...*

I knew from both my research and experience that movements are rare (though talked about quite often) and they are generally found within the nonprofit sector, not the business sector. For the leader of a national, rapidly-moving-into-an-international business to state he wanted a movement instead of an organization really got my attention. I leaned over to whisper into Norma's ear that I liked this guy and that he was well worth listening to for more insight into dōTERRA®. Later she told me she had been on pins and needles waiting to hear my reaction to the founders and what they had to say. She felt relieved after I whispered my brief thoughts to her.

This convention took on a whole new dimension for me. I began to look for any signs that the leadership of dōTERRA® was committed to building a movement or to see if they were just giving lip service to an exciting buzzword. With each speaker, I looked for consistency of what they said with conceptual elements of a movement. In all of the founders and the other corporate speakers, that consistency I was looking for existed. I had begun the movement vetting process. This may sound pretentious on the surface, but it is my belief that there exists a responsibility for all of us to go through a vetting process of any organization, group, club, or team to determine that entity's worthiness of our participation and effort of our time before we join that group or organization. As I have stated earlier, I've attended hundreds of conferences and seminars and though my goal has always been to come away with at least one good idea or concept from each I attended, it always means sitting through meetings. At this dōTERRA® convention, I found myself looking forward to each new topic, each new speaker, and finding more information and concepts than I'd ever had in any other single convention. I had never been to any convention or conference that had so captured my attention.

It was in this convention, the fall of 2013, when David Stirling stood in front of thousands of people and said that if he had his choice, he would prefer that this be a movement and not an organization. This statement revealed to me and the rest of those in attendance a whole lot about Stirling's heart. The rarity of a for-profit company seeking to use the process of a movement to achieve its objectives is extreme – kind of like the rarity of hens' teeth. There are currently no other start-up for-profit companies engaging the principles of movement as a key component of their business venture. There have been a few organizations whose leadership has attempted to incorporate movement into their existing company, but it has been met with limited and in some cases no success. This is an astounding uniqueness in dōTERRA®.

It just may be that David Stirling, the other founders, and corporate leadership were in the same situation that NASA scientists faced after President Kennedy publicly announced in 1961 that we would be putting a man on the moon by the end of that decade. When Kennedy announced this, there wasn't any plan in place to achieve the lofty goal that he proclaimed. In fact, in 1961 there was only a small fraction of the number of people (the handful were all seated in the front row of the venue during Kennedy's presentation) necessary for this moon walk to happen employed and there were even fewer materials and facilities. But you know the end of this space and moon story —

Several years later, when the lead space scientist was asked the question of how he got the scientists to think outside the box because no person had ever stepped foot into outer space prior to this date, his answer was remarkable. He said getting the scientists to think outside the box was not the problem, they were already used to doing this; the problem was that there wasn't any box to start with, so they had to create plans for a venture for which there was no box; no foundation upon which to start and build.

This is almost the same situation for dōTERRA®. Stirling makes a statement, the founders confirm their commitment, and the field force is trying to create a way to produce the desired results. Pursuing the mission of changing the world of health and wellness by means of a movement wrapped in a for-profit venture had yet to be defined in the field. At this point in time, the field force is still looking to achieve the desired results yet they're continuing to use tools and programs inside the box. Instituting movement principles for dōTERRA® extends the opportunity to follow dōTERRA®'s lead in the industry in the same fashion as they have redefined the quality of essential oils and they have redefined and tweaked our residual income model. dōTERRA® essential oils redefine the therapeutic Essential Oil industry; and dōTERRA®'s compensation plan is generous beyond the inside-the-box thinking of MLM companies. dōTERRA® is pioneering in those ways. Yet, there is still work to be done on implementing movement principles to facilitating the changing of this world's health.

Dr. Hill stated from the stage of the 2015 dōTERRA® annual convention that "dōTERRA® is a non-MLM company in an MLM industry." He also stated that "dōTERRA® is a science company" and yes, dōTERRA® utilizes a multi-level marketing and sales compensation plan in order to advance the mission. To be able to share these essential oils in the most effective way, a sales model was needed that would facilitate a personal essential oil experience, provide education on the value of essential oils to the mainstream consumer on an individualized and

> *... non-MLM company in an MLM Industry...*

personal one-on-one basis. This would mean taking essential oils out of the boutiques and getting them into the hands of family caregivers who would normally not be exposed to essential oils. Therefore, the founders of dōTERRA® recognized that a residual income compensation plan would support the word-of-mouth and personal education model required to help people understand the unique value of their therapeutic oils. The Multi-Level Marketing compensation plan fit the basic needs for these purposes. However, they knew they'd have to make some significant changes to the 70-plus-year-old MLM financing model in order to accommodate the advancement of their mission through a movement.

The traditional MLM model of financing is focused on paying the highest percentage of compensation to those on the top level of people in a team and with the lowest percentage of income paid relative to those who are at the deepest levels. That traditional model wouldn't promote engaging, educating, and retaining people to continue to use essential oils that dōTERRA® executives preferred as a starting point in their wellness journey. Remember, the mission of dōTERRA® is to help change the health and wellness of people around the world. To do this there would have to be some way to encourage people to continue to use the oils and continue to be educated on both the oils and how to be in charge of their own health and wellness. Therefore, dōTERRA® inverted the financing levels, by paying the highest percentage of compensation at the deepest level. This provides an incentive for people who have decided to be essential oil and wellness educators to work through others as teams. This incentivization promotes stability and longevity and it partially explains why dōTERRA®'s persistency of users of the oils is so much higher than traditional MLM companies. The other part which explains the higher persistency of dōTERRA® is the emphasis on people, the Wellness Advocates, Wholesale Customers, and prospects. The monetary incentive promotes the adage that people do and pay attention to what they get paid to do and to what is paid attention to.

Now, this next part of the financing model that dōTERRA® utilizes is a format for movement; the Power of 3. Through the use of the Power of 3, Wellness Advocates who have decided to build a business are rewarded financially. By using this model, dōTERRA® is promoting and advancing the philosophy and process of movement through multiplication. Multiplication is the engine which runs a movement. dōTERRA®'s Power of 3 model encourages and supports their Wellness Advocates to spend time getting to know, educate, train, and impact their Wellness Advocates who are key leaders and the many more Wholesale Customers.

We can impress people from a distance as is evidenced by all the self-help books and seminars available in the market; yet we see little to no change in the lives of those who read these books and attend these seminars. It is only when we get close to people that we impact them in ways that will change their lives, and, in turn the lives of those around them. By getting close to our key leaders, our Wellness Advocates need to learn and develop themselves into being the person who has something to offer their key leaders. This will mean that the Wellness Advocate and the

Wellness Advocate's key leaders will need to change and grow. This is where the traditional MLM training, tools, and programs are not adequate. Just as dōTERRA®'s essential oils are unique to the world, there needs to be training, support, education, and the tools necessary for the Wellness Advocates of dōTERRA® to grow that is unique. But the Power of 3 doesn't stop at one level of key leaders. The Power of 3 provides the structure for the key leaders to know, educate, train, and impact their key leaders, who in turn will do the same for their key leaders. This is multiplication! It is not duplication. The difference between multiplication and duplication is addressed in the chapters on Perpetuating the Movement and Principles of Multiplication.

The old MLM financing model that has been uniquely adapted and changed by dōTERRA® allows for an individual approach of working with people on a one-to-one and small group basis as opposed to retail or corporate marketing. For dōTERRA® to develop this particular residual income model for their Wellness Advocates allows for the most rapid spread of advocacy and therefore the greatest opportunity for impact on our world. Plus, this compensation plan of dōTERRA®'s is the most generous in the marketplace to those who do the work of educating the world regarding these highly effective oils and products.

So, why does dōTERRA® continue to be labeled as an MLM even though it is in reality intended to be a science company, a movement, a non-MLM company in an MLM industry? It stems from the use of the MLM financial/income model even though in its tweaked form it is a unique model in the market place and doesn't fit the traditional MLM income model. Secondly and perhaps the most pervasive is from the field force leaders and a majority of the Wellness Advocates themselves. For all of their well-intended efforts, they continue to promote MLM training, tools, and programs as well as promote themselves as part of an MLM company.

As I state this last point about Wellness Advocates and MLM, I am doing so from the perspective that we have a mission to accomplish and in order to accomplish this mission we will need to remove as many stumbling blocks as possible from the paths of those we encounter. This includes those who have already been exposed to dōTERRA® and have decided they didn't like the MLM tactics with which they were confronted. Yes, I've heard all the proponents of the MLM industry say that we've got to embrace and be proud of this industry. This is not an argument against the MLM industry or those who continue to espouse the values of the MLM tools and programs.

However, dōTERRA® is unique and it has a unique mission to accomplish. It doesn't matter whether I embrace and am proud of what the MLM industry is and does; that is not the point or the issue. As Wellness Advocates who are committed to building a movement in order to accomplish the mission, we need to lay aside anything which will hinder people from listening to our message. Unfortunately, calling dōTERRA® an MLM is a detractor to the majority of the mainstream market we're seeking to influence and impact in order to help change the world of health and wellness. It is our job and our responsibility as Wellness Advocates to remove as many barriers and hindrances as possible in our communication with others, not to attempt to convert their thinking by convincing others of the value of Multi-Level Marketing. This is not to hide dōTERRA® but expose and uncover it's true and authentic purpose; to change the world's perception and practice of health care. The excitement of dōTERRA®'s residual income stream should be and is a great advantage for many people; just don't get confused between the residual income stream and the mission dōTERRA® has committed itself to accomplishing. We, as Wellness Advocates should and need to pull in tandem in the same direction as the founders' vision and in which the founders are taking dōTERRA®'s corporate home office – a science company focused on changing the current health and wellness paradigm. If we, the Wellness Advocates won't and don't pull with dōTERRA®, then it's like hitching two horses together with only one of the horses listening to what the driver is directing. Eventually the team comes apart.

Listening to dōTERRA®'s founders, dōTERRA® is a science company first, having a mission to change this world, using a direct sales compensation model, and having a strong emphasis on the growth of individuals. Even so, dōTERRA® corporate is not actually a direct sales company or a multilevel marketing company. Defining dōTERRA® as either of these two marketing approaches to fulfilling the mission is limiting to the movement and is a short-sighted view of what is actually taking place. dōTERRA® is a hybrid of the direct sales sector, the health sector, the science sector, and a movement all within the for-profit business sector and as such deserves the same unique description and representation as the essential oils dōTERRA® produces and makes available to the world. If we, as Wellness Advocates do not get past this point in our thinking, communicating, and acting as MLM proponents, it is my fear that the founders' view, mission, and movement are in jeopardy. The MLM process and training of duplication uplift in words only a person's unique talents, strengths, and behavior while the training and tools promote everyone to become like the leader of the MLM duplication model which hinders and squanders who we were created to be. It is through multiplication, not duplication, that we have the freedom to encourage and help people grow as they were endowed at birth for greatness and success. It is through the concepts and the implementation of these concepts of movement and its multiplication model that dōTERRA®'s full success can be achieved throughout the world.

Up until now, those who have experienced the life-changing effects of dōTERRA®'s Essential Oils have only had the tools employed to market and sell these oils that are based on the direct sales model of marketing and sales. The direct sales model of marketing and selling is based on a 70 or more-year-old approach to sales which has been statistically proven to be more ineffective than effective and its use has been discarded by those in the professional sales world. Additionally, the MLM industry has been closely researched with findings of between 1% and at most 10% of those enrolling being able to earn any measurable net income. So why do we want to use the training, tools, and tactics of an industry that is more unsuccessful than successful, and by this I am not just talking about financial capital, I'm talking about human capital? Why do that?

Within this book, I've provided some alternative models, concepts, and tools that accomplish the objective of giving people a personal experience with the oils while facilitating the growth of each person through their talents and strengths. Even though I've used the phrase "alternative," these tools for movement are more mainstream than what are found within the narrowly focused sector of multilevel marketing. Additionally, you'll find these movement models and tools are based on science, empirical statistics, as well as successful experiences of millions of people in all walks of life and business sectors. These models, concepts, and tools provide platforms on which a movement can be built, the mission can be accomplished, and lives changed for the better.

2
Movements

> *It has only been in more recent times that Movements have become of interest enough for scholars to begin research to define what a movement is and how it works. However, Movements of one purpose or another have been around for centuries. For our purposes, I'm using a composite of what others have sought to define, my research, and my personal involvement and success in movements.*

Why Movements Begin

A Movement begins when someone or a group of people determine there needs to be some form of change to occur which will fundamentally shift current values and culture within a society toward a new vision. More often than not, this person or this group of people are so focused on this need for change and on their belief that the vision they have developed is so instrumental for this change to occur that they are willing to sacrifice incomes, homes, reputations, and possibly even their lives to further their cause. It is because of this identified problem or need to be filled that almost all movements are found in the nonprofit sector.

> *Movements begin in order for change to occur.*

The for-profit sector is focused on making money by providing a service or product which will make life easier for those who can afford the cost of their product or service. Nothing is wrong with this. In fact, it is what has been the foundational backbone of this country and it is what has propelled our country into the forefront of financial success acround the globe. The nonprofit, or sometimes stated as not-for-proft, or charitable organizations are not in the marketplace to make profits. They may provide a service or products but are not allowed by law to be in competition with the for-profit sector, so there is careful and diligent supervision by both the government and the organization to steer clear of this competition.

Yet, recently, there have been a small number of for-profit organizations who have seen the advantages of using the process of a movement to further their mission. These entities began as organizations. Their leaders, looking for and hoping to improve the objective of the organization as well as improve the work environment for their employees, have begun to apply various elements of a movement within their organizational structure. This has been met with some success. However, the underlying obstacle to overcome is the necessary

Change comes at a high cost regardless of the price

change in mindset of their middle and lower management staff. To shift from managing things to leading people is a daunting task and for those in a bureaucratic position of management, this change makes for a fear-proned environment for them. It isn't that their positions are being threatened. It is that those in management positions must change. And change comes at a high cost regardless of the price. As a result of this resistance to change by the middle and lower management team, these organizations whose upper management leadership have attempted to integrate movement into their organization, have met with some, but limited, success. This doesn't mean they need to give up their efforts. But it is something for all those in organizational leadership positions to consider before making this transition. This approach is changing an established and firmly entrenched organizational structure which is highly resistant to change. Whereas, an organization which begins with the elements of a movement established at the beginning of the venture will meet less resistance to building a movement. This is why nonprofits that are driven by mission, not money, have an easier time of pursuing and applying the process of a movement to their mode of operations. The nonprofit needs to maintain a constant vigil against the encroachment of their organizational structurue taking over the movement in the name of advancement. This encroachment is similar to the frog that has when placed in a pan of cold water that is slowly being warmed until the frog is boiled.

Elements of Movements

Movements are driven by vision. Movements are dynamic, so they are continually evolving to further the vision and tweak the vision as societies and cultures change and as previously established goals are achieved. Vision should and must be the rallying cry for all of the team. It is easy for any of us to lose our focus on the vision because of the myriad of problems facing us every day. Yet it is the vision to which people respond and are called within movements that transcends the daily mundane chores we all face. It is vision, indeed, that not just compels us, but impels us to travel onward.

Movements are about people, moving them to action, challenging them to change in order to further the mission derived from the vision, and building relationships with others who will see the need for this change and who will be intrinsically moved to connect with and join the movement. The relationships with others and the continual need for those involved to grow personally and to grow in the mission are the lifeblood of movements.

Time becomes a factor in how the movement grows, because depending upon the vision, the change which needs to take place may occur over years, a lifetime, or generations, until the completion of the vision is actualized. Since the mission to fulfill the vision needs time for the team members to grow and for the evolution of the mission to adapt to the moving target brought on by the impact of the efforts of the team, there needs to have built into the strategic plan a balance between the immediacy of solving the problem identified by the leaders and time for individual growth of the members of the team. The need of pursuing the vision and changing the lives of those the movement affects is today, yet the work to complete the mission of the movement will likely take years to achieve. It takes a lifetime to build an oak as well as to build people.

Movements will use a variety of strategies, may change their organizational structure, and/or may create a hybrid of current organizational structures in order to meet the demands of furthering the vision. There isn't any "right" strategy to which everyone must conform. Various strategies may need to be employed in order to further the vision of the movement.

However, it is important to point out at this time that the most successful movements utilize a decentralized strategy and organizational structure. This decentralization is considered an open system of management and control where there is more flexibility for the staff to provide input, make decisions, and help drive the mission of the movement. When centralized strategic models have been implemented either at the beginning of the movement or as new leadership assumes control, a critical and fundamental change in organizational structuring occurs. These centralized strategic models of management prefer the management of things over the development of people.

> *It's easier to manage things than it is to lead people, but it's only as people grow that things change*

Management of things is both easier and more cost effective in the short-run than the development of people. And the change from a decentralized people driven movement structure to a centralized task driven structure is most vulnerable when there is a change in upper management due to the founder(s) retirement or passing.

When the founder(s) initially conceived their vision and determined the decentralized people driven movement would be the best management model to follow, the first obstacle to overcome would be to identify and influence upper management of the value and perpetuation of this management model. The second obstacle is when the founder or founders retire, become disabled, or pass away. The perpetuation of the vision of the leader and leadership of the movement is a combination of being taught, that is educated, about the positive values of movement and it must be caught. No matter the amount of teaching of movement, unless there is a catching in the mind and the heart of the following management leaders, the movement will die. If the concept of movement in the company's strategic management model isn't caught the movement will die, possibly slowly, but it will die.

With new leadership there is always the peril of losing the vision and the heart of what made the company great. And when there is new management there is always change. The question is will the change be for the better of the company or the betterment of the new leaders? New leaders face the scrutiny of boards which demand more results. These leaders often view their position as a stepping stone for further advancement in position and income. These same leaders often seek to bask in the glory of leaving their own legacy and mark for others to admire. All of these impel these new leaders toward a shifting away from movement into a centralized organizational structure driven by accomplishing tasks but not building people. And the once great vision of the founder or founders dies, so does the movement and the company is no longer the success it once was.

Another difficulty for nonprofit organizations is in education and training of leaders. The majority of leadership management overwhelmingly consists of the education and training of leaders through colleges, universities, and self-help seminars which perpetuates the mindset of building the structure of an organization and plugging people into the advancement of the organization. These new leaders don't have any training, background, successes, or practical application of what it takes to work through balancing the focus of the movement through the application of an organization. Preparing the next generation of movement leaders and planning for fluid organizational support to the movement in the transition from one generation of leaders to another must be at the center of the founding leader's mind if the mission and the movement to fulfill the mission are to be successful. This means there needs to be hands on training and imparting of vision and mission by the founders and those disciples who have mastered the balance between movement and organization. Additionally, the successor leaders need to be alert and beware of falling into the trap of pursuing success through the advancement of organization over movement.

In summary, the defining of a movement hinges upon a need for change to occur; the vision generated by and through an individual or a group of individuals who are willing to commit to the movement and if need be to sacrifice their lives and fortunes for this change; commitment to the vision; and people who are attracted to and will attract others to the mission. It is the vision which

> *Vision drives movement*

drives the movement and it is the people who provide the movement with the lifeblood necessary for success.

Delineation of the Elements of Movements

There are elements or components of movements which help identify the movement from other types of ventures.

- Identification of a Cause – defining a societal problem which needs to be corrected for the betterment of the society

- Development of a Vision/Mission – developing a solution or set of solutions by a person or a group of people who believe they can positively affect and even fix, cure, or rid society of the identified problem.

- People attracted to and willing to work for the cause – people catching the vision for the change, who believe in the solution(s), and who are willing to invest their lives to affect this change.

- Decentralized Organization – Operating with the central focus that people and mission are of the utmost importance to the success of affecting the change, the most successful type of organization being the decentralized organization. The decentralized organization will:

- have in place the people whose talents, strengths, skills, and experience prepare them for a particular job

- allow for people to have the most authority over their own areas of responsibility

- provide flexibility for leadership to pivot their marketing and financial responses in order to meet the needs addressed by the vision,

- be most conducive for leadership development in order to further the vision, and

- be the most open platform for expansion to new areas, acquiring and utilizing non-traditional forms for leadership development and the perpetuation of the mission beyond the lifespan of the founders.

3
Building a Movement

Process not Program

Movements are a process not a program. A movement focuses on the individual needs of both the people within the movement and those whom the movement serves. Movements serve people, but not by analyzing them as statistics to be measured. Movements don't focus on the materials or the methods used to further the mission, though it will use both to achieve its objectives. And this next point is critical to better understand and differentiate between movements and organizations; movements focus on the people, organizations focus on the materials and the methods. This last point is so critical to what separates a movement from an organization and the loss of which causes the devolving of a movement into an organization.

> *Movements focus on people; those being served and* **those serving.**

When a movement begins, the founders have in the front of their minds and at the center of their hearts the need to fix some problem that is harmful to people. They're driven by their need to overcome this problem because of the damage it is causing to people. Get it? It's people that drives them; it's people who motivate them; it's people who are in need of this change for which the founders may be the only one(s) who can positively affect this change.

Everything about the founders of a movement and their efforts to overcome this problem is centered on the need to help others. This is one of the key reasons why, when shortly after the birth of this movement of dōTERRA® when people begin joining, there is little and in some cases no training in programs, skills, and materials. It is all about solving the need for and affecting change for others.

However, as the movement gains in strength, people, and time those people who were some of the early joiners have risen to leadership positions. These leaders may still have the heart for furthering the mission, but their head says there needs to be better and more organization. These same people may have studied the latest management theories and techniques and have come away with the understanding that to further the mission of the organization

> *People are more important than things*

it is easier to manage things than it is to develop people. However, when this occurs, the movement begins its downward slide toward becoming just another organization that started out with good intentions. This is why the last point is so crucial to the growth, health, and success of the movement. People are more important than things.

Multiple not individual

A crucial element of building a movement is that, if a movement is properly understood, the process is multiple not individual. No one person has, as a leader, all the right qualities necessary for leading and serving others; therefore, it is critical to have those involved in the movement learn from a number of people and sources. If those within the movement are not exposed to other leaders and sources, it is very easy for those in the movement to develop a dependency on the leader(s) without themselves ever becoming leaders. Additionally, those within the movement will emulate not only the strengths of the leader(s) but they will also take on that leader's weaknesses, which limits others by the leaders' own limitations. The value of a team is crucial to a movement. Knowing the strengths of the individual team members allows the leaders to focus on building on strengths not on trying to correct weaknesses. Two things occur when leaders focus on a person's weaknesses – the person gets frustrated and at best the person has now become mediocre. Building on the individual's talents and strengths within the team paves the way for the next crucial element of a movement; multiplication.

Multiplication; not duplication

Multiplication is the lifeblood of a movement. Multiplication breathes life into those who have committed and dedicated their lives to the fulfillment of the mission. Multiplication creates, builds, and fosters an environment of each person's unique talents and strengths so that this diversity creates a synergy beyond what is taught through

> *Multiplication generates a synergy built on people's talents and strengths*

duplication. In order for the mission to be successful, there needs to be an equipping of the team and this is where the use of tools and training techniques relative to movement enters as a means to serve both the mission and the people committed to the mission. These tools and techniques are to sharpen, hone, and empower the people in order to further the mission. However, the emphasis and the continued focus during all of this training is on the unique talents and strengths of each individual. The tools and techniques play a secondary role in the building of the team.

> *Multiplication! It's a paradigm shift in our mindset*

Multiplication provides the focus of the mission for team members to utilize and facilitate the tools and techniques by applying them to situations as they arise. The tools and techniques become the servant of the people and the mission. This is the shift in mindset that is so crucial for the leaders in the field and team members to grasp, learn, and apply. Always staying focused on the mission, not losing sight of a changed world through changed people. Successful multiplication, and thereby a successful movement, relies upon understanding and applying this little, though significant, shift in our mindsets. This little mindset shift creates a significant paradigm shift in our thinking which flows through to a major change in the way we conduct our work and business. This is multiplication! And multiplication is not the same as duplication.

Often uninformed or misinformed individuals will try to pass off multiplication as a semantical variation of duplication. Nothing could be further from the truth. Multiplication focuses on the people, their preferred way of working (behavior), and their strengths. Duplication focuses on the materials and the methods. Materials and methods will be used by multiplying leaders to help others become leaders; however, the multiplying leader's emphasis and focus is always on helping others become leaders. Materials and methods are interchangeable while people are never interchangeable. In duplication, people become interchangeable and the materials and methods must be followed and obeyed, with no deviation. Valuing people more than materials and methods empowers people to become multiplying leaders and is crucial to the success of each person and to the movement.

Additionally, duplication has as its central theme the concept of building a clone of the one doing the training and/or leading. Duplication robs people of their strengths, diminishes their light to this world, and limits their capacity for excellence. Notice I didn't identify financial success. Duplication can bring financial success in the for-profit world, often at a rapid rate of growth; however, with this comes the cost of losing the uniqueness of the strengths of individuals. It is important to remember that duplication is based on all becoming like the person promoting their particular pathway to success which is in effect, cloning. This is where great movements have floundered, failed, and fallen by the wayside. Attempting to make everyone just like a select few sacrifices the strengths of all of the individuals in order to gain the advancement of whatever is on the agenda of the one doing the cloning. Don't let the glitter of duplication fool you into believing that you're really helping people become their best because in effect what you're doing is attempting to make them over into an image of yourself. And if you think on that long enough it's likely to give you nightmares, because they won't just pick up your strengths, they'll also pick up your weaknesses.

Those leaders who have learned and taken unto themselves this change in mindset employ the significant difference between multiplication and duplication in their working with others. They will utilize materials and methods employed by others but will do so by picking and choosing which of these tools will best be suited for the further development of an individual's growth. Further, multiplication requires time for the leader to get to know team members, to spend individual time with each one through a coaching and/or mentoring process. A leader using multiplication will know individuals on the team well enough to know which tools will work for each of them. And this is where one of the great tenets of leadership becomes all important to the leader. We can impress people from a distance, but we can only impact them up close. All of this presupposes the leader to have taken the time to master the tools of materials and methods in order to serve and support their teammates.

> *We impress people from a distance; we impact people up close.*

Tools for building a Movement

There is an old saying, "If we understand the 'why' any 'how' will work." That phrase may not be the best use of the English language but it might help in understanding the relationship between the tools we need to identify and utilize in a movement and the training of the team which advances the philosophy of people as more important than things, inclusive of money and numbers which form statistics.

Any research on the subject of tools, training, and programs will reveal that while lip service is given to the value of people, their substance is designed to move products, gain financial success, build a bigger organization, etc. There isn't anything inherently wrong with the substance of this training, but it is a subterfuge of what the presenters have as an agenda that is wrong. The tools normally used for providing the knowledge and skills to better educate and train people can be used, but there needs to be additional education and training on the building of people. This is where most if not all movements have failed. It is easier to find these training programs and then implement them through an off the shelf "plug and play" means of self-training. This works in limited success in for-profit organizations. I specifically have stated that even within for-profit organization, these training methods have limited success because we know that 67% of all employees surveyed (by Gallup and reported in several places, including cbsnews.com in a March 31, 2017 article entitled, "Why So Many Americans Hate Their Jobs!") report they are unhappy, underchallenged, and underappreciated in their work. There needs to be more of a hands on, discipling approach, to working with the team members of a non-profit organization. Additionally, there needs to be more relational and people building training. This means finding tools which are designed to identify how people prefer to be treated, finding people's talents, strengths, and passions, and then building an environment conducive to their individual growth around each person. These tools are available in the marketplace. However, because these tools are designed for the unique and authentic development of each person, the implementation of these tools requires coaches who specialize in their use. It will also require the leaders and team members of the movement to develop a paradigm shift in their thinking and acting from the instantaneous expectations of change to a realistic application provided through the tools knowing that change takes time because we're dealing with people not machines. Some of these tools which are the easiest to learn and apply are found in this book which combines SOCIAL STYLE® and Gallup's Strengths. Another tool is DiSC®, which is not found in this book. These tools for building people are in addition to the need by team leaders to train and build skills with their team members.

4

Perpetuating the Movement

A Movement's Leader is a Servant Leader

Another element necessary for the building of a movement is for the leader to become a servant leader, an authentic leader. This role of being a servant leader is rooted in the leader's development of servanthood, not of power in the traditional sense. If the goal for the leader is to encourage and support the development of others into their full potential as leaders, then servant leadership becomes an indispensable quality in the life of the leader. In order for the movement to perpetuate or go beyond the life of the founders, there must be the development of others who will take on the role of servant leadership in the same vein as that of the founders. If this is not a critical element that is purposefully developed, focused on, and implemented within the movement, then the movement will die within the second or third generation of leaders because it will have devolved into an organization whereby the original mission, and ultimately, the movement will be lost.

The lack of servant leadership is where most movements and organizations wipe out. Without this element of servant leadership embedded into the character of the founders and leaders of the movement, the people involved quickly become convinced that the only reason they are valuable to that founder/leader is to further the program. What the people are seeing is not servant leadership but power and ambition to further the program at the expense of the people, both those served and those serving. People see power over the people, not power collectively with the people. Those who have joined the team will see their roles as cogs in the wheels of the machine, which serves mainly to further the agenda of the founder/leader.

When the leader has developed a mindset and the character to be a servant leader, then the relationship between the leader and the follower is: "I'm the leader, you're the trainee, and we will work together for you to build your character, your skills, and your talents/strengths so that you will become the leader." There is a major shift in the approach and outcome when working with others with this leadership mindset. The leader has moved from, "I'm the leader, you're the follower; now do this, it'll be good for you" to "I'm the leader and together we're going to find your talents and strengths to develop you as a leader." The shift moves from "me and others," to "we" who are in this thing together. This is the key component to avoiding what happens in 99% of all organizations; the plugging of holes by the leaders in order to achieve their own goals. Individuals lose value when their purpose is to plug a hole so the leader can achieve their goals. And when the individual sees they have lost value, the movement and organization will lose the individual.

When we begin working with others, there are two basic things to focus on as needs in the lives of those whom we serve and on which you will never lose when you are working with others. First, everybody needs to be loved. Second, everybody needs to be served. If you as a servant leader will focus on these two needs in the lives of those whom you lead, you will never lack for leaders prepared to lead and for the mission of the movement to perpetuate. People tend to follow those who love them and serve their needs, not those who try to lord it over them.

> *Everybody needs to be loved; everybody needs to be served.*

Movements and Organizations

In looking at the building of a movement, it is almost impossible to do without also identifying both the value and the limitations of organizations. Movements alone and without the benefit of some type of organizational structure tend to be hobbies from which little or no societal benefits occur. The value of the organization to the movement is to serve the mission and the people of the movement. The limitation of the organization is that the same organizational structure which serves the advancement of the mission and the people can become the structure which strangles and kills the movement. Leadership of the movement becomes critical to the success of the movement. It is those in leadership who have to continually weigh and balance the value of people against the value of the program. People and

> *"Take away my people but leave my factories and soon grass will grow on the factory floors…Take away my factories but leave my people and soon we will have a new and better factory."* Andrew Carnegie

program become the weights on each side of the movement scale. Without people who share in the vision and mission of the movement, the movement dies and the organization takes over.

Consider this analogy: A movement is the purpose for which a train is assembled. It is the written statement but unseen driving force which dictates the number and types of cars to be used, the number of engines necessary to pull the cars, and the tracks on which the train moves. If the purpose (movement) of the train is forgotten or ignored, then the train will have a great number of cars, engines, and track, but will have lost its value for the purpose it was intended. Movements will use organizations to further the cause however, organizations do not have the ability to use or facilitate a movement for its advancement. Historically, no organization has ever successfully evolved into a movement; but movements can and historically do devolve into organizations which kill movements. But some organizational programs may work and, indeed, must be utilized to support the movement.

It is a fact that it is easier to manage an organization than it is to lead people. Those who become the leaders of a movement eventually give way by losing focus of their vision, retiring, or dying. In most cases, those who follow and are then left in control of the movement generally don't have the same heart for the mission, they become enamored with statistics as more

> *"You can take my factories, burn up my buildings, but give me my people and I'll build right back again."* Henry Ford

important than people, or they've just found it is easier to manage things than it is to lead people. This can and generally does occur in the second or third generation of leaders. Sure, the written mission is still in play but the new leaders have figured out a way by which they can alter, ignore, or amend the vision for the movement. When this happens, the organization has taken over the movement, then the movement is on the downward path of destruction and will eventually disintegrate. Sometimes it is better that the movement dies, making room for a new movement with its new or revitalized vision and mission to take the old one's place.

The Mathematics and Principles of a Movement

For years now, people have been illustrating the difference between multiplication and addition of people through the use of purely mathematical examples. For those of you who have not as of yet had the opportunity to learn of these examples, I've done the math for you in the examples. And, for those of you who have seen the examples and in some cases, may have used the examples to explain your point or have become jaded as to the value of the examples, I've got an insight that you might be interested in learning. This insight comes from years of both using and practicing these examples and I hope will be worth your wading through the examples to get to what I've learned.

One example is to offer to pay someone to work for you for 30 days in one of two ways: 1) to be paid a salary, or 2) with the first day's pay being a penny with wages being doubled each day from the previous day's wage for those 30 days. Which would you take? Would you be willing to take an established salary or would you be willing to take an evolving income? If you choose the second offering, the earnings for the first couple of weeks are pitiful but hang on.

On the 30th day your wages, **for that single day**, would be, $5,368,709.12.

Pretty impressive for a day's worth of your effort. Your total income for the 30-day month would be, $10,737,418.23. An interesting note at this point is that on the 31st day of work, should you extend the contract one more day, your income would be $10,737,418.24 for that 31st day alone. That's just a little more income in one day than what you earned for the entire prior 30 days.

Meanwhile, for those who chose to work for the same pay the first day as the last, your salary would have to be $178,956.97 per day to equal the $5,368,709.12 earned on the 30th day; and it would have to be $357,913.94 per day to equal your total income for the month.

It's not likely you'll ever get hired for either of these figures! The entire point is that multiplication is slow in the beginning, but as it progresses, it gains exponentially, whereas, addition remains static and it must have an exceedingly large amount of investment to begin with and have that same amount of invested capital to sustain itself for the duration of the whole time frame.

And NO, this is not the insight I was referring to. You'll have to keep reading.

Another example comes from the evangelical world - explaining the difference between doing evangelism and discipleship. Evangelism by itself is similar to addition. If we had an evangelist who would be able to speak to 1,000 people per day and allowing the evangelist to take 2 weeks of vacation per year, the question becomes, how long would it take for the evangelist to reach every person in the world with his message? Here's the math; 1,000 people per day, seven days per week, 50 weeks equals 350,000 per year. Today there are approximately 7.5 billion people in the world. Presuming the world's population would remain static, it would take the evangelist almost 21,482 years to reach each person.

Moving on to multiplication. Instead of the evangelist, we began with just me. My objective is to find one person to train to be an evangelist, work with him for 6 months, preparing him to be ready at the end of 6 months to find a person of his own to train. At the end of the first 6 months each of us finds a new person and prepares the new person to be ready at the end of 6 months and so on. Using this method, it would take 16.5 years to reach 7.5 billion people and would even allow for the continued growth of the world's population to 8.7 billion.

Think about it, to reach the world for Christianity, work for over 21,000 years or 16.5 years, which would you choose? Which method is more effective and efficient?

These examples are the reasons why most people are enamored with multiplication. There isn't any wonder in my mind as to why so many people, good people, want to achieve success by using multiplication of numbers. It is so much faster in the long term than any other method. Yet, if multiplication is so much faster in the long run, then why it is that we have not, as of yet, seen the success the numbers of the multiplication model indicate we should be seeing?

Now comes the insight. Most people have either (this is the most likely reason) never been informed about or, (very few people fall into this category) have forgotten or been sidetracked from the most important principle of multiplication. This first and most important principle is that **People Are the Method!** I'll be explaining this principle later in this chapter, but for now it is important to understand that for all of the discussions, seminars, talks, etc. about multiplication, instead of looking for better people, there is a constant search for better methods, programs, and training. All of these are important and even necessary for the success of using multiplication.

People are the Method

However, it is only when we learn, understand, and apply the principle of people being the method that we really begin to see multiplication soar. How do I know? I've been privileged to have both participated in one multiplication of a movement which achieved the desired goal and I have led another such movement a few years later. The key to this success? The most important principle of all of the principles of multiplication, that people are the method, was the principle I focused on every day of my life since I learned this profound truth. This principle was the framework used for changing me and it was only through my being changed that the use of multiplication to achieve the movement's success was fulfilled.

Multiplication, by definition, has a greater effect on the end result than does duplication. Multiplication is achieved through a process. Duplication is achieved through programs. The term multiplication is not interchangeable with the term duplication; the processes are different, and the end results are incredibly different. It is not just a difference in semantics. Multiplication employs a process based on a set of principles. The cornerstone of these principles is to know, understand, believe, and apply the value that people are the method; that people are more important than the programs designed to train people; that people are more important than short-term goals; that it is people whom we serve.

> *Getting people done through work; work is the means by which people grow*

However, in order for any of us to have this principle as a cornerstone in our lives, we must be willing to change our mindsets from what we've heard and seen most of our lives. This change in mindset will cause a major paradigm shift in our lives and in the lives of those with whom we work. I've been calling it changing our mindset; in reality it is changing our heartset. For anything to become permanent in our lives it takes more than a change in how and what we think. Granted it begins with our thinking, but it is only when we travel the greatest distance we'll ever travel, the distance between our head and our heart, that we truly change our mindset. It is changing our mindset and our actions (heartset) from getting work done through people to "getting people done through work." Therefore, this mind - and heartset - must occur so that every person with whom you meet is seen as a person who might become a teammate of yours and who will join us in changing this world. They are not potential customers, sharers, or builders! They are potential teammates! This perspective is crucial to how you'll view the seven stages of the sales process and how you'll view each person with whom you come into contact relative to your dōTERRA® business. If each person you meet and share the life-changing effects of both the oils and the heartset of health and wellness is a potential teammate, then as you build this part of your relationship you'll have established the foundation of how you'll work with them when they do become teammates. Also, as I build on this different way of thinking and acting, now is a good time to understand a significant and extremely important change in your heartset.

Not everyone with whom you share about the oils will become a builder, though all of them who do become Wellness Advocates (WA) or Wholesale Customers (WC) will become teammates. This means that some will buy the oils and use them as they either can

> *Each person we meet is a potential teammate to changing this world's health 'heartset'!*

afford them or as they see the value of their use. Some will buy the oils and share with others and some of those shared with will become WAs or WCs, but the WA doing the sharing may not want to build or develop this as a business. Some of the WAs will want to build a business to the point where they will be able to pay for their own family's use of the oils but not go beyond that. Some will see how using the oils and sharing the concept of changing the world fits what they've been looking for and will want to build this as a business. And still others may have any combination of these and other thoughts I haven't identified. Statistically, we know that approximately 94% of all dōTERRA® members are going to use the oils for a number of different reasons other than wanting this as a career. This means that approximately 6% of the Wellness Advocates will become successful business builders as defined by dōTERRA®'s published statistics. So, don't view each prospect as a potential anything other than a potential teammate. Once they become a teammate they will begin to self-identify what their involvement will be and the extent of their involvement.

One of the most common and recurring questions I am asked by WA builders is how do they and how should they work with each person on the team. The answer is simple; you can't, so don't. However, through multiplication, you can positively affect every person on the team with your philosophy, values, and concepts. As your team grows and it becomes impossible to work with every team member, you can pour your life into **five to eight** others on the team who in turn will pour their lives into **five to eight** others, who will pour their lives into **five to eight** others, etc.

Two thoughts here. One is that when you are working a full-time job outside of building your wellness business, you may only have time for **one to three** people into whose lives you can pour yours. That is okay and, in fact, it is perfect. If those one to three in turn pour their lives into the same number of people or if their work schedule permits, they can work with a few more, through multiplication you will still be growing your team; and it will grow exponentially.

The second thought is regarding "span of influence," commonly called "span of control" in the business world. I've changed the wording because every person who becomes a Wellness Advocate is an independent business owner. This means every Wellness Advocate can listen to the advice, system, program, etc. of their upline or to some other person and choose to act upon it or, they can choose not to act upon the advice, system, program, etc. As independent business owners, we have the right and the power to make our own decisions. We are not under any obligation to comply with what an upline or downline or crossline person tells us to do. This is very different from being an employee, in which case you either comply with the supervisor or boss or suffer the consequences of being fired, demoted, passed over for promotion, or having your wages stagnated. Therefore, for our use as Wellness Advocates, the term is not a "span of control," rather it is a "span of influence." In order to have an impact on those with whom you work, your span of influence should never exceed eight to ten people. This last statement contains an important and crucial point. There is a huge, no, a humongous difference between having an impact on people's lives and impressing people. The closer you can get to a person, the greater the impact you'll have and make on their lives. We can impress people from a distance, say a stage, a webinar, a seminar, a Facebook Live, or a book. It is only when we get close to the individual that we will have and make an impact on their lives. Yet, with all of this said, the number of people an upline person can successfully influence is proportionate to the success of the upline and the downline person. However, if the upline person is attempting to work closely with too many downline people, that is a number of people beyond the span of influence, both the downline people being closely worked with will suffer as will those who aren't and who will feel neglected. If the leader works with too few, then the downline people will tend to form cliques and will fail to become multipliers for their teams. They've created a club. By the way,

> *We can impress people from a distance; we impact people when we get close to them*

if the upline person thinks they can do a great job with more than eight to ten people, they will fail to provide one or both of the two things people have always felt needs for in their lives; **to be loved and to be served**. Through multiplication these basic needs will be met.

When most people hear the word "multiplication," their impression is that this is just another currently fashionable buzzword word for duplication. Or they think in mathematical terms of one person (the leader) enlists 3-5 people to engage in the work, each of whom will enlist 3-5 more people, who will enlist 3-5 more, ad infinitum. Both thoughts are wrong! The concept of multiplication is comprised of foundational principles which, when applied in the building and training of others, leads the trained to be empowered, authentic, consistent, and seen as having integrity. Additionally, because of these principles, multiplication is multi-dimensional, meaning it is more than just adding numbers; it's creative and allows other opportunities for each individual member's own creativity; it's empowering, uplifting, and promoting of exponential growth.

Duplication does exactly what the word implies; it makes a copy of an action or a program. That is, it copies what is already in existence with the goal being to exactly replicate what already exists. Cloning would be a good synonym. Duplication in and of itself is not a bad concept when it is applied to inanimate creation and re-creation of manufactured items such as furniture, cars, boats, bicycles, and you name it, things which need to have a high degree of sameness.

However, when duplication is applied to people and the programs used to build and train people, duplication becomes an albatross around the neck of those being built and trained. People should not and cannot be duplicated. People weren't created to be duplicated, replicated, or cloned. When speakers or authors teach others to say exactly what the speaker or author says, to do exactly what the speaker or author does, to do it when the speaker or author says, and to do it in the same way as the speaker or author does, many things, most of which are negative, take place. But the underlying, deadly inference is that unless everyone becomes exactly like the speaker or author, they cannot be successful, and they will fail. If this is contrary to what you've been taught, if it makes you mad, if it goes against the grain of what you believe…good. Because now is the time to consider this of yourself: I have been uniquely created; I have unique talents and strengths; I have a unique way I prefer to be treated and to accomplish work; being true to who I am provides me and others with a consistency which defines my authenticity. Then, why would I want to throw my uniqueness, my authenticity away just to allow myself to become a duplicate of someone else?

5
Principles of Multiplication

Principle # 1

Individuals are the method.

Everyone is looking for better methods, better training programs, better tools. In fact, take some time and look up these words (methods, training, programs, and tools) which are associated with building and training people and you'll find 95% if not more of all programs are designed to plug people into whatever is being promoted. If you're going to use multiplication as your process, then you've got to start with the principle that it is people who are the method. It is the significance and uniqueness of individual lives that will effect change, not the plugging of holes. Besides, we know there is a great difficulty with trying to plug a square hole with a round peg or vice versa. There are inevitable leaks and a constant friction of trying to fit in.

Over the years I've discussed this principle of multiplication vs duplication with hundreds of people. Responses vary very little from one person to another. The people with whom I've discussed this principle all give an intellectual assent or agreement that multiplication makes sense. However, as soon as they begin to work with those who are interested in growing and becoming multipliers themselves, this principle is often forgotten. The glory of gaining results with programming people wins out. And there isn't any question that in the short run the pumping up of programs is easier and gets quicker results.

Plugging people into a program is much easier to manage than it is to coach individuals. Coaching individuals requires that the coach gets to know the person, to observe how that person prefers to be treated, how that person acts and reacts with others, and the coach must identify the individual's talents and strengths.

Additionally, the coach must have been trained on these principles in order to be effective. This is crucial, especially in our world today. Today the perspective is that if I've attended a seminar or watched a video I am an expert. It's the "I've stayed at the Holiday Inn Express..." mentality. Coaching requires people desirous of being a coach to be properly trained themselves in order to be able to train others and be effective. This coaching of people is almost always slow in the beginning, but as the coached people begin to believe they have talents, strengths, capabilities, and a future grow exponentially, validating the concept of multiplication. Multiplying my talents and strengths with those unique talents and strengths of others talents and strengths becomes a multiplication factor very different from using duplication of myself into 3-5 others who in turn will duplicate 3-5 others, etc. The multiplication factor I'm talking about is identifying, knowing, and applying my talents, strengths, and behavioral preferences with those of

Coaching requires the coach to be people trained in order to be effective

others on the team and then strategically coaching them to become their best selves.

Principle #2
Find individuals who are teachable!

And more importantly, find those who are teachable by you! The world looks at people based on their appearance, their sophistication, their education, their circle of friends and more. We need to look at the heart of each person who says they want to be builders, multipliers. Do they have a sincere yearning to join us in helping to change the world of health care; are they honest; have they demonstrated a willingness to work and work hard; are they willing to admit their mistakes; do they desire to serve the needs of others – even to the detriment of their own time and interest; can they be brutally honest with themselves when it comes to who they are and what they want; and are they willing to let go of those things which detract from the goal they have set for themselves? Remember, you're not looking for everyone to do this. In fact, this leadership group is a small minority of builders in comparison to the large number of people who will join your team as oil users. You never know who among your oilers might step up one day out of the blue and state a newly found desire to build.

One last word on this section. I discovered over the years in working with many on our and others' teams and it should be obvious to all who are truly entrepreneurially minded; but it is nowhere to be found in the concepts manuals of many of the existing programs in use today. Wait for it! Here it is:

This is an entrepreneurial business. And, further, this is a sales business.

I've found that many people who have started out with the best of intentions wind up saying this builder-multiplier concept and role is more than they bargained for. They are still excited about the oils, holistic living, and wellness, but they prefer to nurture those who are on their team, add a person here and there, and continue to grow in their knowledge and application of the oils and the science behind them. But they are not in the 6%. They are wonderful, valuable, and precious team members. They are just not entrepreneurs.

> *This is an entrepreneurial business…this is a sales business*

It isn't that they have become unteachable. In fact, this may be the farthest thing from their thoughts and actions. It's that they are now recognizing this is a sales and entrepreneurial business and they either no longer have the heart to do the work or they have come to the realization they never had that heart desire. Some are even afraid to admit they sell oils!

Principle #3

Do they have a heart desire to help change this world of health care?

In the Bible, Paul says, "this one thing I do." The modern translation that so many have today is, " these 40 things I dabble in." For your business to be successful to the highest levels, this must be a call, not from me and the pages of this book, though I am hoping to direct your thoughts and actions toward this call. This call has been laid out by the founders and corporate leaders of dōTERRA®. Are we willing to ask ourselves the tough questions regarding our seriousness to answer this call, of the need for this work, of our being able to lay aside 39 of those 40 things we would dabble in to focus on just one thing; answering the call of taking the essential oils, dōTERRA®'s essential oils, to the world and making an indelible impact on how all health care is practiced? Are you?

Principle #4

Concentrate upon a few.

Look for your leaders, identified as those who not only respond to the prior three principles, but who also take the initiative to further the mission. dōTERRA® has established a format for us to follow through the Power of Three.

> *People are the method to success...not programs*

However, after you've been in the business a while, your actual leaders may not be in your original first level of builders. Many times, the top 3 people with whom you've kept the enrollments are not the ones who want to continue to build-multiply. Then what?

Normally, in order to save our incomes, we plug the holes by adding new people; we make purchases which will provide us the Power of Three income; we beg, plead, get angry with, and attempt all other sorts of manipulative motivation. And we find ourselves right back at the same starting point at the beginning of each new month.

Solutions: Continue to focus on the first three principles. Always be adding new people whom you've enrolled and keep the enrollment. Continue to work with those who at the moment aren't ready to go beyond their current level of activity because in most cases they are still committed to the mission and to the personal use of the oils. Remember, people are the method, not the programs. Work at your own paradigm shift of believing and applying the principle that people are the method. By changing your heartset and wrapping your mind and heart around the value of people as more important than programs or things, you will attract more people like yourself.

> *If you're not adding new people to your team, you're going backward*

Principle #5

Don't neglect the masses.

Look for ways to get the message out to larger groups of people. Remember, 94% of all members are consumers or are those who are willing to share minimally. They are and will always continue to be the body of our business and income. Don't conform to the thinking that many have by calling them "squatters." They are your team members. You may be able to gain rank by working with them to change the enroller and you'll retain their volume; however, only by adding new people will your volume soar, and it's in this volume where the depth of your income will come.

- Encourage your leaders to truly lead in the area of recruiting new people. This is one of the most important and successful ways you can build those on your team and to keep them involved in learning.
- Continue having classes, but don't only have Intro classes. Change up the content and topics. People on the team are the ones who will find others who will in turn find others, who in turn will find others.
- Work with your leaders to attend expos and other wellness events where you can get the information out to the masses. Do booths or exhibits. Do a demo for a craft group or a report to a literary club.
- You can sponsor or work in conjunction with one or more others to sponsor events in your local area. Be a servant to your community through these sponsorships. If you decide you'd like to either sponsor or be part of sponsoring an event, find people on your team who have strengths who can facilitate success for the event. A couple of strengths to consider are Strategic (not to be confused with strategic thinking), Activator, Achiever, Arranger, and Maximizer. But, please, don't look at these few strengths as the only strengths which will be necessary.

- Remember, every person's strengths are built on their talents. Look for the talents within the strength themes because the talents you and your team may need might be found in those strengths I've not identified. These strengths are within the Executing, Influencing, and Strategic Thinking domains.

- But, you're also going to need some folks on the team who have strong Relationship Building Domain strengths. These people know people. These people are connected to the community. These people bring a warmth to the team that creates momentum in a well-oiled machine, but due to their talents and strengths, they are more focused on the relational element of working with people and they may need your help with structure or placements.

- In other words, know your team members' talents and strengths; know their behavioral preferences; rely upon what each person brings to the organizing of the event; and lastly, respect the strengths of others, being willing to work through the differences of viewpoints to achieve the common goal. Working together, let's change the world's view and practice of health care.

6

Relationships: Foundations of Success

> **Earl Nightingale**
>
> "Dean of Personal Development," Author of "The Strangest Secret", and co-founder of NightingaleConant
>
> *"Relationships form the foundation, the all-important base, upon which motivating, leading, and building others takes place."*

Good relationships are more than something we want in our lives; they are something we need...even to those who pride themselves on being loners, self-sufficient, or independent. We all need good relationships to be our healthiest, happiest, and most productive selves. Good relationships strengthen all aspects of our lives. Zenger – Folkman, in their book, "The Extraordinary Leader," repeatedly state that a person's ability to develop interpersonal skills (relationships) when connected and used with any one of the other elements of leadership (character, focusing on results, personal capability, and leading organizational change) is the leading component and therefore the main reason for a person's success at work. Good relationships, and thereby, supportive relationships, strengthen our health, our minds, our spirits, our bodies, and our work.

However, we are not born with these good supportive relationships. We have to work at them. Granted, some people have what appears to be an easier time building relationships with others, yet, even they fail from time to time. Healthy relationships don't come to any of us automatically. Healthy relationships take time, effort, energy, and practice. The more we know how to build good relationships with others, and the more we practice applying this knowledge, building and strengthening our relationship and social skills, the more healthy and productive our lives will be.

The foundation of all successful relationships is good communication. As a freshman in college, I, along with the rest of the freshman class, was required to take a basic English course. It was in this basic course in English that I first learned about effectively communicating with another person through my writing and my speaking. I learned that when we listen and speak with each other we do so by filtering everything we hear and say through our personal experiences, persuasions, beliefs, backgrounds, etc. Therefore, it is important for each of us to eliminate as many of these filters as we can by communicating with words and actions to which the listener/reader can best relate. I learned that communication is the foundation of connecting with others and it is the foundation of building successful relationships. Though I learned this as a college freshman, it wasn't until much later that I learned an additional truth in communication. I learned that 70 percent of all

> *"The ability to develop interpersonal skills is the leading component and therefore the main reason for a person's success at work."*
>
> The Extraordinary Leader by Zenger Folkman

communication is non-verbal. Facial expressions, gestures, eye contact, posture, plus the volume and tone of voice empowers others to 'hear' more than the actual words that are spoken. We need to watch what people do more than what they say. Our and their actions speak louder than words.

At the heart and core of what we do as Wellness Advocates is the building of relationships. We are constantly coming into contact with a variety of people. Those people come in all shapes, sizes, backgrounds, ancestral lineage, God-given unique characteristics, family values, and more. Our ability to build good, vibrant, and healthy relationships with others depends first on our ability to effectively communicate. We need to find a means, a tool, which will help us improve our communication with others. Our success depends on our ability to develop proper relationships with each person with whom we come into contact.

> *TRACOM states that 70% of all communication is non-verbal and 20% is tone.*
>
> *In the movie, Hitch,* Hitch states that *90% of all communication is non-verbal (60% non-verbal and 30% tone)*

Most of us may not consider communication and relationship building as much of a skill as it is a common practice. However, communicating with others and the building of relationships with others is not only an art, but it is rooted or founded in science. The ability to put the art and the science together becomes a skill. The better we are at knowing and then applying the science of communication, the more effective we will be at developing the art of effectively relating with others.

Each of us has a way in which we like to receive information. This is called a filter. Whenever we're in communication with another person or group of people, we listen to what is being said through our own personal filter. Though we generally discuss this filter as if it is singular, in actuality it is collective, meaning it is made up of a number of things. Among those things which affect our filtering are personality, love language, talents, strengths, gifts, birth order, and I'll let you finish the list. It is quite extensive and can become very complex. Just remember, each of us is unique and there is only one of us in this world.

One of the most helpful tools in communicating with others and building relationships is actually a model built on the science of communication. I was first introduced to this model in my professional career as an insurance agent. This model is based on a scientific study providing information on how I and others prefer to be treated, giving key insights into how prospects and clients preferred to be approached, worked with, and inspired. It is based upon a scientific study of observing the behavioral preferences and patterns of how people interact in asserting their preferences and their responding to others through these same preferences. This is not a personality test or a color or shape test, or any other of the myriad of tests designed to talk about personalities. It is also not a study of body language. This is a behavioral study, with over 60 years of research as its foundation, based on observing the actions of others and from these observations being able to know how to approach and interact with others. The simplicity of this model is that we can adjust to others in a matter of minutes in order to communicate and build a relationship with them based on how they prefer to receive information.

Social Intelligence

There are three elements to Social Intelligence: our Behavioral Style; our Emotional Intelligence; and our Mindset. Of these three, our Behavioral Style is the easiest to identify and assess. Whatever setting we are in, whether it be work, family, play, etc., how we interact with others and how they interact with us either moves us forward or slaps us backward in our relationships. Whether you read, listen to a podcast or other audio device, attend a seminar or conference, or some other means of learning, you'll find that a vital element of becoming a great leader is the development of interpersonal skills or as it is becoming known today, social intelligence. In the book, *The Extraordinary Leader*, by John Zenger and Joseph Folkman, they identify interpersonal skills as the second most important element in a person's growth as a leader; the first is that of developing our character. However, their telling us that we need to develop this second element of becoming a leader and becoming more effective is only the beginning. What I have found over the years is that the simplest, most effective tool to help me treat others as they prefer to be treated, create win/win situations with others and myself, and give me insights as to how to quickly pivot in order to adapt to

> *There are three elements to Social Intelligence: Behavioral Style, Emotional Intelligence, and Mindset.*

others is a Behavioral Style Model called SOCIAL STYLE®.

Though I've found this model to be extremely helpful in building relationships, both in personal and working environments, it is not magical. Some of the people whom I have taught to use this model have seen some magical results, but the model itself is not magical. What this model does is provide a means of communicating, interacting, and discussing with others how people prefer to be approached and treated in our working with them. It provides us a language with words based on observing instead of judging people. Instead of floundering our way through relationships not knowing why a person behaves in a certain way, we can know and then act instead of reacting. Instead of throwing our hands up, shaking our heads in disbelief, and muttering to ourselves, we can gain insight into their actions, find it easier to forgive or ask for forgiveness, and be supportive rather than find ourselves infuriated or frustrated.

Remember, in order for us to build better relationships with others, we first must improve our own communication skills. Improving our communication skills means learning the how to of communicating, not just the why, in order for us to build positive and healthy relationships with others.

I was teaching a class on building relationships using the SOCIAL STYLE MODEL™ and had just introduced how this behavioral model works in building relationships with others. In the front of the audience and to my right were two sisters. I noticed them because both of them could comfortably sit in an overstuffed chair and still have extra room. However, while I was presenting the why, what, and how of the SOCIAL STYLE MODEL™, neither of them joined in the numerous discussion times during the presentation.

It was some time after I'd opened the discussion for participation with the attendees on what their behavioral style is and what their thoughts were as to their style that one of the sisters looked at me and said that she'd been married to her husband for 15 years. Continuing, she said that during all those years she'd thought that her husband was angry with her and she kept trying to figure out how to please him. After learning about the four Styles, she realized that he hadn't been mad. Through the class, she'd learned that he has a Driving Style and that his preferences are geared toward action and results, while she has an Amiable Style and her preferences are geared toward relationships and support of others. She shared that for the first time in their marriage, she felt at peace knowing that he wasn't angry with her; he was just focused on getting things done. A few months later my wife had the opportunity to meet and have dinner with both sisters and their husbands. When she returned from her trip, Norma and I discussed how the couples were doing. She reported that both couples shared how valuable the class had been to them and that because of the training they were communicating better because the sisters had gained valuable insight into the behavioral styles of others and how they prefer to be approached and treated. Though this training is not intended to be marriage counseling, the spillover in that area can be great!

Part of my presentation on SOCIAL STYLE® is putting people's behavioral styles into the context of how the culture in which we were reared has an effect on us. The impact from our culture creates filters of the words and phrases we use and the experiences we've encountered. What this means is that culture can impact how we express ourselves and live out our Style. We feel that in order for us to fit into various social settings we need to comply with the perceived norms. Sometimes when this occurs we attempt to change our Style to a different Style from our own in order to fit into the perceived socially acceptable Style. Stop! Don't do that! Your Style and its preferences are unique to you. You're born with a Style preference and during the early years of growth you continue to build on this Style. Therefore, when we attempt to change our Style to fit in, we're denying the way God created us, and we lose the value for which we were designed. We are no longer authentic, and we may be viewed as phony.

> *Your SOCIAL STYLE® is what you were born with and that Style's preferences are unique to you.*

During the mid-point break of one of my classes, one of the participants sought me out to share that she'd been the wife of a pastor for about 35 years. According to her, the culture within most churches of her denomination for the wife of a pastor is that she should be more compatible with the Amiable Style. During the first half of our class, she'd learned that the Style in which she was most comfortable and which she could identify was the Driving Style. Continuing, she shared that all of her life she had identified with pursuing and achieving goals, but that as a pastor's wife, her role was to build relationships and to have a more "submissive" place in the church. For the first time in 35 years she felt she could be who she was created to be and not have to try and be someone else. She was freed to express her behavioral Driving style as she was designed to be.

Working with Style awareness is all about building relationships with others, and this includes the relationship with one's spouse. We meet a person, fall in love with them, marry them, and finally get the privilege of living with them. And as all the marriage counseling books and counselors tell us, the living with the love of our lives isn't always what we thought it would be. This living with someone is where the rubber meets the road and real friction can occur. It's here in the everyday friction of life where identifying and adjusting to our spouse's Style becomes a tool to help us appreciate and love our mate, even during difficult times. Because of the work that my wife and I perform, it is an almost daily part of our conversations that the topics of communicating effectively, building relationships, and appreciating people for who they are, are discussed. Through the SOCIAL STYLE MODEL™, we've been able to gain insight to how we think, feel, and act differently from each other and to appreciate and laugh through our differences. Our use of this behavioral model has been a great tool for us and our relationship and for our relationships with others.

> *Working with SOCIAL STYLE® Awareness is all about building relationships.*

In every class I teach, there is a generous sprinkling of anecdotes about Norma's and my life together. This means I share both the parts of our lives in which we are in complete agreement, such as our relationship to Christ, living a principle-centered life, our focus on the family, etc. However, it also means I share those parts of our lives in which we are opposite of each other; she is a gregarious people person, while I'm more comfortable as a loner; she's sees everything through a filtered lens of positivity, while I look through a critical thinking lens; she is a "foodie," which means she loves to experiment with putting ingredients together, while if it's hot and brown and/or a hot dish (of any color as I'm not particular when it comes to hot dishes), I'm happy. We are different! But, we love the differences in our lives and we love to laugh at those differences and grow in our relationship because of our appreciation of these differences.

...some people are foodies, others aren't

At another class on SOCIAL STYLE®, there was a couple whom we'd briefly gotten to know and with whom we were beginning to develop a friendship. During the class there was limited participation on their part, but they seemed to be intently listening and learning. A few weeks after the class, Norma was in a conversation with one of the daughters of this couple. In that conversation, the daughter asked Norma what it was that I'd taught. Norma briefly explained about Style Awareness. The daughter then said that after having attended that class, her parents had positively made some changes in their lives and in their relationship with each other. She went on to say she saw her dad much more affectionate and patient with her mom and that her mom was more open in expressing her feelings. The daughter expressed her gratitude and thanked Norma for being involved with her parents and extended a thanks to me for teaching the class.

Prior to my learning about the SOCIAL STYLE MODEL™, muddling my way through relationships was more the norm of my life than the exception. The following is an illustration of this muddling, though fortunately for the clients and for me it worked out positively; I got lucky.

Very early in my career as an Estate Planner, in fact, it was my very first estate planning opportunity, I was meeting with a husband and wife, a farming couple. It was in the late fall and after the corn had been harvested which meant both of them had time to see me. They were a young couple with two boys ages 10 and 12. We were meeting in their kitchen of their house, which was a typical setting for my working with farmers on their estate plans. Their kitchen was a typical farm kitchen, meaning it was a large room which served as a kitchen, a casual eating area, and an office for their farming operation. The kitchen table had been slid against a wall with three kitchen chairs and a secretarial chair for sitting. The husband, Dan, sat on the secretarial chair on one side of the table and Sarah sat across from him on one kitchen chair with her broken leg propped up on another kitchen chair. I sat in the third chair, between them. After about 45 minutes of general conversation, I finally screwed up enough courage to open the subject of estate planning for them and for their children's future. I began by asking some demographic questions, and after learning how to spell their names and the names of their children, and confirming their address, I opened with a question which would provide me with what was foremost on their hearts regarding this planning.

"Dan, if you were to die before you could complete your plans for your family, what would you like to have happen with your farm?" Without batting an eye, he leaned across the table looking directly at his wife, pointing at her, and said, "I don't care what happens as long as she doesn't get a penny!" Shocked, I was staggered by what he'd just said. All I could do was stare at him. Pulling my eyes from him, I looked at his wife and saw she was as frozen as I was. His face was flushed, with his jaw set, appearing immovable. Looking around the kitchen for something to help me either escape the room or change the subject, I saw something that caught my eye. On the stove, within my arm's reach, was an empty cast iron frying pan. Reaching back as if to grab it, I looked at him, then at Sarah and said to her, "would you like me to hit him or do you want to hit him?" He exploded by pushing himself in his rolling secretarial chair away from the table out of the kitchen and into the mud room, about 8 feet away.

> *"I don't care as long as she doesn't get a penny!"*

There we sat. Dan looking at me. Me looking at Dan, then at Sarah, then back to Dan, then back to Sarah. Since Dan had pushed himself so far into the mudroom that Sarah couldn't see him, all she could do was look embarrassed and mad at the same time. Realizing it was my meeting and that I'd better figure out a way to salvage the situation, I knew I had to come up with something to break the uncomfortable silence. I looked over at Dan and I said, "I'm not going to hit you, because I believe you've got a reason why you said what you said. Come on back over to the table so we can talk about it."

After a few more seconds of his sizing up the situation, Dan slowly used his feet to pull himself and his chair back toward the kitchen table. Having just met them for the first time that day, I figured the meeting could well be over and I would soon be back in my car headed home. During the time it took Dan to get himself and his chair back to the table, a question popped into my head. So, I asked, "Dan, do you love Sarah?" Without hesitating for a moment, he fired back at me, "Of course, I love her! I'm taking her on a Caribbean cruise in February and we'll be gone for three weeks!" The tension of what was said earlier was now replaced with confusion on Sarah's face and in my mind. Looking squarely into Dan's face, I asked my next question, "Ok, but if you love her, there must be some reason why you just said you don't want her to get a penny!" Replying, he said, "Because, if I die before she does, she's going to marry some jerk who's going to take the farm away from my boys and they won't get anything. I'm working for the benefit of the boys to have a future on this farm!" I looked at him and thought to myself, "I think Sarah may have already married the jerk," however what I actually said was, "Dan, if we can solve that problem for you and your boys so they will never be left out of any inheritance, would you have any problem making sure that Sarah is well cared for?" His response, "Of course, that'd be ok with me. I do love her; I just don't want the boys not to be able get what I've spent my life working for." We finished the meeting and continued the estate planning process.

The purpose of my sharing this story with you, besides the fact I like to tell stories, is that had I been knowledgeable of the SOCIAL STYLE MODEL™, I would have been able to determine Dan and Sarah's behavioral styles. Seeing Dan as a Driving style and Sarah as an Amiable style would have clued me in as to how they preferred to be treated and interacted with each other. I would still have asked the question about the future of the farm, and Dan might still have responded in the same way, but, I would have been better prepared for Dan's answer. As a person who has a Driving style of behavior, I would have recognized that he was looking for the immediate need to get results. I might have been able to diffuse Dan's answer with follow up questions designed to soften the impact of his words and gain clarity of what he really meant. Additionally, I might have been able to pivot to Sarah, who, having an Amiable behavioral style, was focused on relationships and being supportive to Dan and the boys. Knowing this, I would have been able to help her recover from her hurt feelings and possible thoughts of divorce.

As I said, this was very early in my estate planning career and I had yet to learn about behavioral preferences and patterns that people have. At the time, I was able to defuse a very explosive situation, but it was more by luck than anything else, and it was certainly not by any science. It was a few years later when I first learned about behavioral styles and a couple of years after that that I began instructing people on how to use behavioral styles, in order to build better relationships with others. Over the years, I've had lots of practice in using this behavioral model, not only in my career, but also with my family and friends. The more I practiced the better I got at identifying others' behavioral styles.

Most of the time we're judged on or by our behavior. We use judging words to describe what a person did - which means we've drawn conclusions as to their motives for doing something. This leads to building walls within ourselves or around others. Instead of this judging, what if there was a way for us to observe a person's behavior, make a non-judging assessment of their actions, and be able to continue to build a positive relationship with them? If we could do this, we could significantly reduce many of the barriers in our communication with others and move forward in building positive relationships with them. We can't know what a person is currently feeling and thinking or what a person has gone through in his or her life, but we can identify behavioral actions in a non-judging manner. David Stirling, CEO and founder of dōTERRA® has said, "If we treat each person we come into contact with as if they are either in a crisis, have just come through a crisis, or are just entering a crisis, in the majority of the situations, we'll be correct."

Most of the time we are incorrectly judged on our behavior which leads to wrong conclusions and relational walls built

What we need then is a model which will help us get past the judging. We need a model which will provide us with a better language to describe and explain how a person prefers to be treated. The model that I've found and which I use as one of five coaching models for working with others is called the SOCIAL STYLE MODEL™.

The SOCIAL STYLE MODEL™ was created in 1964 by Dr. David W. Merrill who was an industrial psychologist and university professor. Dr. Merrill began researching predictors of success in selling and management careers, finding through empirical studies, that people tend to display consistent, observable behaviors. Further he found that those who are exposed to his findings can consistently agree on words to describe each behavior. This work became the foundation of the SOCIAL STYLE MODEL™, and was the beginning of The TRACOM Group.

There are four styles of behavior as identified by this behavioral model: Driving, Expressive, Amiable, and Analytical. Each of the four Styles displays positive and negative characteristics when working with others, and research shows that people of any SOCIAL STYLE® can be successful in any profession. A person's SOCIAL STYLE® is not inherently good or bad. In fact, we are born with a specific style of behavior. Additionally, there are 25% of the population in each quadrant. No one style is better or worse than another. And no particular style is a predictor of success or failure.

> 4 Behavioral Styles
> *Driving or Dominant*
> *Expressive or Influencing*
> *Amiable or Supportive*
> *Analytical or Cautious*

Often I have people tell me they can see themselves in all four quadrants, depending on the situation they're facing. This can be true. However, a key point to know and understand regarding the SOCIAL STYLE MODEL™ is to look at each of the four quadrants as four rooms in a house. Throughout the day, we go in and out of all of the rooms. However, there is one particular room that makes us feel comfortable, where we can feel the most like ourselves and can relax. It's the room where you can sort of kick your shoes off and just be you. Similarly, in the SOCIAL STYLE MODEL™ you'll find there is one quadrant where you feel the most like you. You can see yourself more comfortable in one of the quadrants than in the others and once you've taken some time to better understand each of the quadrants, you'll be able to best identify with that Style of behavior as being your dominant Style.

Knowing our own Style is important. In fact, before we can ever begin to better understand how others prefer to be approached and treated, we need to know how we want to be approached and treated. If this sounds a whole lot like the Golden Rule, it actually is a "how to" on applying the Golden Rule to every person, every day.

The Golden Rule is generally stated as, "Do unto others as you would have others do unto you." This particular quote is the most easily recognized and comes from the King James version of the Bible in Matthew 7:12. Other versions have a similar but different way of saying the same thing. For years we've heard this taught from Sunday School classes, church pulpits, seminars, lectures, and have read about it in countless books and even heard it quoted in movies. And just about every time when the explanation as to how to apply this to our lives is given, it's from an erred perspective [that as we treat others in a way we would like to be treated it will be the way they really want to be treated.] This erred way of applying the Golden Rule doesn't take into account our needing to learn anything about the other person. Usually my actions toward the other person are based on my understanding of me and of what and how I'd like to be treated. But if the other person doesn't want to be treated in the same way as I do, or if this way of treating them doesn't connect with who they are then, what do we do? Approaching the Golden Rule from this erred perspective opens the door for us to fail to connect with others and loses the value of what was being taught.

> *The SOCIAL STYLE Model™ provides us with the "how" to live the **Golden Rule** as it was meant to be lived.*

However, if we have a way, by observing a person's behavior, to gain some insights on how they prefer to be approached, communicated with, and treated, then the value and lesson of the Golden Rule comes to life. By using this behavioral style model of working with others, we're given a 'how to' in identifying and working with them in a manner in which they can positively respond to our approach. And we really can do unto them in their preferred Style as we would have them do unto us in our preferred Style.

However, the real value of my knowing my Style and of my being able to identify other people's Style is in my being able to know how they prefer to be treated so I can adjust my Style to better work with them in theirs. When I do this, I am reducing what is called "noise" in communication and lowering the tension between us which makes for better interpersonal communication and thereby brings more effectiveness in my working with them. The measure of how effective I am in working with others is called Versatility. Because we're born with a particular behavioral Style, our Style is automatic and habitual to us. Unlike our behavioral Style, Versatility behavior requires conscious awareness and effort. Versatility is not something we're born with; we have to practice being aware of our Style and others' Styles; how our Styles interact with each other, and what works to make more effective interpersonal relationships between or among Styles. Usually we have to make a concerted and continuing effort to become good at Versatility.

> **Real Value of Style Awareness**
> *To know my Style and to identify other's Style so I can treat them the way they prefer to be treated.*

My use of the SOCIAL STYLE MODEL™ over the past 30+ years has laid the foundation upon which I've been able to grow and help others grow in the building of relationships. This model has provided me the ability to move away from the judging of others and into assessing them through their behavior.

When I first learned about dōTERRA® and the vision to change the world's view of health care, I realized that in order for this to be successful it would have to be built on relationships. Additionally, I realized that a great many people would be coming together to join the founders in accomplishing this vision. All of us, and those who have yet to join us, have wide and diverse backgrounds, growing personalities, varying social and economic structures, and unique talents and strengths. In order for this large number of diverse people to positively build relationships with each other, there is a need for them to have a tool or tools which teach and train them to be more effective in their communication with each other. The <u>SOCIAL STYLE MODEL™</u> provides this education and training. This model can elevate people and the building of relationships, where we no longer judge others, but we observe their behavioral style. By doing this we can set aside preconceived ideas of others, prejudices, and opinions and build positive relationships toward mutual success.

Gaining knowledge, applying this knowledge, and then developing the skill of being able to identify the behavioral styles of others is the foundation of the SOCIAL STYLE MODEL™. This gaining of insight into our own Style preference is the first part. The second part of the SOCIAL STYLE MODEL™ is the concept which connects a person's Style with those of other Styles. This is called Versatility. Being able to develop Versatility is what leads to interpersonal effectiveness.

Versatility

Defining Versatility; it is a measure of a person's interpersonal effectiveness of supporting and respecting the Style of others. Style behaviors are automatic for us. Versatility requires conscious awareness and effort in working with others. This is a skill which comes only after continued practice. Style awareness training provides us the information to identify another's Style and in knowing what and how that person prefers to be approached, respected, and treated. Versatility is:

- having the ability to know our own style and how we prefer to be treated

- through observation of another person's behavior to know how they prefer to be treated, then

- choosing to focus on meeting the needs of the other person while

- staying within our own style.

A person with low Versatility is characterized by two things:

- focused on and choosing to meet their own Style needs

- not understanding or not paying attention through observation of the other person's Style needs

Some ways to identify low or poor Versatility is:

- when the person is abruptly interrupting others

- telling them how things should be done
- wanting things done their way
- not allowing others to voice their thoughts or finish what they're saying
- moving the discussion to what they're interested in discussing.

Some ways to identify high or mature Versatility is:
- actively listens to what the other person is saying
- focused on the behavior of the other person
- providing feedback, letting the other person know they are being heard and understood
- checking to make sure the other person's expectations are being heard and met
- addressing the Style need and expectations of the other person

People who have developed and continue to develop Versatility choose to do something for others. The person with high/mature Versatility makes others feel comfortable, listened to, appreciated, and respected. This leads to a productive relationship where everyone comes away from the time together believing and feeling progress was made.

High/mature Versatility can be very effective when first meeting and working with another person. It can also provide the foundation for future and further meetings and discussion. At the initial meeting a person with high/mature Versatility should be able to gain great insight into the life of the other person. By doing so the development of mutual respect and trust is formed. However, just as in our talents and strengths there are three things which can negatively affect a person's high/mature Versatility:

- illness
- exhaustion
- too much stress

This is a good time for me to point out that high/mature Versatility is not a permanent position. Through any of the preceding points we can demonstrate a low/immature Versatility. Therefore it is important to know that to maintain a high/mature level of Versatility, we need to continuously work at managing our health, our rest, and the tension that is in our lives. Developing and maintaining a high/mature level of Versatility is a long-term effort, a long distance run, not a short-term sprint.

There is much more to be discussed and learned about the SOCIAL STYLE MODEL™. Where the real work comes is in the application of what a person learns from this Model. I wish there were time and resources for me to spend time with any or all of you for me to give what I've learned over these past many years. Short of being able to do this, if you or a group of you are interested in learning more about how this Model for building better relationships works and can be applied by you and your team, let me know. There are very few (one or two) books written on this subject and the only method of educating and training others on how this works is through attending one of several seminars. I am a certified instructor in the SOCIAL STYLE MODEL™ and will be glad to discuss a session or a seminar on this for you. (I know this really does sound like a plug, but it is the only way to learn more about this behavioral model.)

The Golden Rule, the Platinum Rule, and...

The **Golden Rule**: "Do unto others as you would have others do unto you."

The **Platinum Rule**: "Treat others the way they want to be treated."

On the surface, they look very different. The Golden Rule appears to be self-centered while the Platinum Rule appears to be other-centered. Don't let the appearances fool you. Appearances can be and often are deceptively inaccurate. They are in this case.

The Golden Rule
It focuses on two elements of working with others:
1. The ability to know oneself.
2. The willingness to do something for others.

Now, digging a little deeper. First, *the ability to know oneself*. This is often overlooked or undervalued. In order for us to really be able to help others, we need to know what talents, strengths, and skills we have which can be of service to others. Without this knowledge as a starting point, we can often do harm or damage to others, sometimes even to the point of the relationship's being irreparable. Examples abound throughout our lives.

Here are a few examples to consider:
- the well-meaning relative or friend who oversteps boundaries in order to "help."
- telling others what to do, even though we either can't, don't, or won't do it ourselves.
- being told that if we try hard enough, believe hard enough, that we can do anything.
- attempting to do something which is not authentic to us because we don't know ourselves, making us inauthentic:
  "Do as I say do, not as I do."

Know one's self by knowing how we prefer to be approached and treated and finding our talents and strengths. Then become a student of developing these talents and strengths into skills which will help you to grow in your capabilities. From this knowledge of yourself and by this, I mean your talents and strengths, you'll be ready to have an impact on others. Don't get caught up in trying to fix your weaknesses; you'll hurt yourself and others because no matter how hard you work on your weaknesses, they will never become strengths. What Jesus was saying is that by taking the time to study ourselves, that is, how we prefer to be treated, encouraged, challenged, motivated, etc. (the process we need to put ourselves through in order to know ourselves) is the training ground for our ability to do the same for others. Once we know ourselves, then we can help others as they prefer to be treated. We need to understand that there is a process we must learn in order to examine ourselves and that same process is what is valuable as we seek to know others in the way they prefer to be treated.

The Golden Rule, per Jesus, teaches that we need to know ourselves first in order to reduce, and hopefully not do any, harm to others. The Golden Rule has laid the groundwork that all people are unique. Once we've begun the process of knowing ourselves, we can apply this knowledge and process to treating others as they prefer to be treated. It is from our growth that we can come alongside others, help them know themselves, what their talents and strengths are, and help them to master the skills necessary for their own unique growth. This is really treating others the way they prefer to be treated, which is what we want for ourselves – to be treated in the way that makes sense to us.

The Platinum Rule
It focuses on one element and makes one assumption in working with others:
1. Focuses on: treating others as they want to be treated.
2. Assumption: we already know how they want to be treated

I am choosing not to go into much depth on this Rule as the internet is filled with a host of people touting its worth. However, when you take some time to research this Rule, you will find a few points of interest. One, each person espousing this Rule as a replacement for the Golden Rule does so in order to sell a book, sell their services, and/or advance their "guru" status. Two, their explanation of the Golden Rule is superficial at best and is often a put down of its no longer being of value. Three, they either take credit for having originated this Rule or, at the least say they are the ones who have the most insight on how it should be applied.

Regardless of the reasoning behind this wanting to replace the Golden Rule with the Platinum Rule, there is one, and by far the most important point in their premise which cuts to the heart of Christianity: It implies that Jesus is not God. It also demonstrates a basic theological ignorance of who Jesus as the Christ is, God; a blatant disregard for the relevancy of Christ and His teaching which transcends time; and it reveals the superficiality of them and their work. This is not the time or the place in which to engage in a theological debate, I am merely offering this as food for your thinking. Don't be so deceived into believing that man has the ability to outdo God by creating their rules while at the same time furthering their own fame, reputation, financial advancement, or ego. And even though I am all for people having the creativity to advance ideas and enjoy financial gain from that creativity, I'm not so quick to throw aside what I believe in order to advance simplistic, superficial research in order to gain that wealth.

And...
There is now a Double Platinum Rule which has been incorporated into what the person espousing this claims are the Three Universal Rules: The Golden Rule, the Platinum Rule, and the Double Platinum Rule. Wow, what's next? The Triple Platinum Rule, perhaps similar to the Triple Lindy from the movie, Back to School starring Rodney Dangerfield?

In summary, when the Golden Rule is properly understood and implemented, there is no need for any other superseding rule to shore up or replace it. The Golden Rule is sufficient!

7
The Genius of You...
Talents and Strengths

> *"Most Americans don't know what their strengths are. When you ask them, they look at you with a blank stare, or they respond in terms of subject knowledge, which is the wrong answer."* Peter Drucker

Anyone who has ever sat across a table or desk from a prospective employer, has heard the directives, "Tell me about your strengths," followed by, "Tell me about your weaknesses." If you were offered the position, generally there would be a brief discussion between you and the employer in which it would be explained that, due to your strengths, you could help fill a need at the company. Then inevitably, about 6 months to a year later, most often during an annual review, your supervisor would meet with you to go over the progress you've made during this time. While you're in this review, your successes would be indicated, however, your weaknesses would become the primary focus of discussion. And with this discussion would be a number of suggestions and directives on how you would need to improve on your weaknesses. Your strengths were there but they were accepted as the norm while your weaknesses were identified as what was hindering you and the company from achieving the company's goals.

Whenever I have been in the position of hiring a new sales person or office person, I've given each person the same directive, "Tell me about your strengths" and "Tell me about your weaknesses." Every time, I got the same types of responses. Generally, their responses fell into broad categories of the work they did but they never told me about themselves; they could define their strengths or weaknesses as they applied to specific duties but they didn't tell me anything about the strengths or weakness they personally had. When I settled on hiring a person, I knew there'd be a lot of work that I needed to do through observing them in action for me to get a feel for their strengths. I knew that behind the work they described as their strengths, lay hidden their real talents and strengths.

> *Observation, (and this takes time) of others is a key element to knowing a person's strengths*

I just needed the time to observe them in action over a long period of time in order for me to find a theme of what they were truly good and gifted at doing. I knew I would need to string together the threads of their unique abilities to find what they did best and what they did effortlessly. By observing them over a period of time I could create a matrix in my mind of their talents. Then through a series of discussions with them, giving them opportunities to explore what both of us thought might be a strength, adjusting what worked and didn't work, together we could bring out their best.

Finding their weaknesses was a whole lot easier. Their weaknesses would emerge all too quickly and over a shorter time. Whenever a weakness would be uncovered, the new employee's expectation of me was that I'd point out their weakness, scold, confront, or otherwise intimidate them, followed by some form of remedial seminar(s), work project, or having to write on the chalkboard 500 times, "I will not do this again." Their expectation was that I'd want to fix them and their weakness. However, in each meeting I'd communicate that I could see their weakness when I hired them. What I wanted to do was build on their talents and strengths in order to bring out their best. Then, together we'd figure out some ways to overcome the weakness without their having to focus on it.

> *Weaknesses are easy to find in others. Focusing on their strengths takes work.*

Most of the time our expectations are that we have to identify our weaknesses and then try to fix them. This is both an inherent trait of people and it is what continues to be taught, trained, and otherwise ingrained into the lives of those who listen to the advice of self-help people. It isn't any wonder that shortly after we're hired, and our weaknesses emerge that we forget the value of our strengths and rotate ourselves clockwise into a downward spiral of anguish, frustration, and resentment.

Anyone who has tried their hand at becoming an independent business owner, or lacked adequate funding to start their own business but longed to be in business, or desired to supplement or replace their income, has probably been introduced to Direct Sales or Multi-Level Marketing. The approach to working with people as taught within these industries is called duplication. The recruiters within these types of businesses are not as concerned with your strengths or weaknesses as much as they are in your willingness to do exactly what they say you are to do through their process of duplication.

Training, seminars, classes, events, and individual meetings are advertised as being centered around the concept of duplicating their processes. These speakers go to great lengths to share, exhort, educate, and cajole their audience as to how unique their programs are and that if those in attendance will only follow, doing exactly what is presented, they will be able to be successful. These same speakers will throw in some brief information that is unique, but the thrust of what is taught are the programs. While giving the illusion that they are preaching the uniqueness of each person, their primary objective is to conform people into the image of their programs or maybe themselves or another highly paid or highly-ranked team member. Some speakers have gone so far as to say that if you will do exactly what they do, say the exact same words, and deliver the words in the exact same manner, that success will be right around the corner.

Duplication conforms not frees the uniqueness of individuals

My challenge to you is, lift the veil! Open the curtain! See the man from Kansas as the Wizard of Oz! See that the words of people saying they are committed to each person being unique and their desire is to build on that uniqueness is an illusion. Their actual practice is that of conforming people into the image of their programs. Granted they have achieved financial success. And who wouldn't want the kind of financial success they tout? However, statistically, less than 10% of the people who follow these self-help speakers achieve a similar financial success. And according to more recent studies on the success rate for those who follow these teachings within the MLM industry, it is closer to 1-3%.

Putting this in context with starting your own business, studies have continued to demonstrate that approximately 30% of the people starting their own business as independent entrepreneurs achieve success outside of the direct sales industry.

Here's something for you to consider as you read through this book. For you to conform to someone else's image, you must have their strengths. And we know that the odds of anyone else having the same strengths as you, in the exact same order is one out of 33 million people. The concept, programs, and practice of duplication and the uniqueness of individuals don't go well together.

> *"Everybody is a genius. But if you judge a fish by its ability to climb a tree, it will live its whole life believing that it is stupid."*
> Albert Einstein

They are incongruent. There is a different concept that does work well with the uniqueness of individuals. It is called multiplication. I discuss this concept in the chapter titled, Principles of Multiplication in Chapter 5.

Does this make the leaders of the Direct Sales or MLM industries inherently bad people? No, at least not any more or less than those who are in the pyramidal hierarchy of corporate industry. Do the methods employed by these leaders help people grow through their strengths? Not unless the people being educated and trained have very similar talents and strengths to those doing the educating and training, and statistically this is a very low probability. Both the MLM industry and the corporate industry have inadequate methods of working with people and helping people achieve success. There is a better way.

The study of strengths is based within the theory of positive psychology which is the study of what is right with people and focusing on their value. Most psychology is based on the deficits and illnesses within people. This newer study of psychology had its roots in the mind of a Midwestern college student from Butte, Nebraska. As a graduate student in 1952 at the University of Nebraska, Lincoln, Donald O. Clifton, asked the question "What would happen if we actually studied what is right with people?" In 1953, Donald O. Clifton was awarded a doctorate in educational psychology. With this question and Dr. Clifton's pursuit of the answers, a new way of viewing people and working with them, a new branch of psychology began to take shape. In 1988, Dr. Clifton's company, Selection Research Inc. purchased and merged with The Gallup Organization. Due to the household name and the integrity of The Gallup Organization's polling efforts, Selection Research Inc. chose to retain the name of Gallup in the merger, creating the company called, Gallup. In 2002 the Gallup Clifton StrengthsFinder assessment was created as an online (www.gallupstrengthscenter.com) assessment that helps people identify their talents and strengths. As of this printing, over 20 million people have taken this assessment worldwide. In 2003, Dr. Clifton was commended by the American Psychological Association as "the father of Strengths-Based Psychology and the grandfather of Positive Psychology."

"The Clifton StrengthsFinder is based on a general model of Positive Psychology, which is a framework, or paradigm, that encompasses an approach to psychology from the perspective of healthy, successful life functioning. Topics include optimism, positive emotions, spirituality, happiness, satisfaction, personal development, and wellbeing. These and similar topics may be studied at the individual level or in a workgroup, family, or community. While some who study Positive Psychology are therapists, a more typical distinction is that therapists focus on removing dysfunction, while Positive Psychologists focus on maintaining or enhancing successful function." **Gallup.**

The last sentence in the quote from Gallup is crucial to understanding the value of the Clifton StrengthsFinder and its results. It is the "maintaining or enhancing successful function(s)" which provides us with the application of what our talents and strengths are and how they are of value to us. Most of us don't live in a theoretical world. We want to know that if we learn something we will be able to apply it to our lives in a

> *Knowing and applying our talents and strengths leads us to being the unique and authentic person we were created to be.*

way that will make us better people; we want to revel in our uniqueness. The Clifton StrengthsFinder provides us this knowledge through reports of our Top 5 Strengths and the underlying talents of those strengths. We want, or should want, to know that what we are choosing to believe of ourselves will provide us information and from the application of this information, the skills necessary to grow into our unique self. And that by growing into our unique self we will be authentic in our relationships and interactions with others. The Gallup Clifton StrengthsFinder assessment is rooted and founded in science, refined and honed through research, tested and proven to be effective through statistical analysis by the millions of people who have taken the Gallup Clifton StrengthsFinder assessment. This is in contrast to what is generally taught in the business sectors.

Too often, the teachings and trainings within the MLM, Direct Sales, and corporate sectors of business approach working with people from the perspective of finding out what people are doing wrong and then attempting to fix it. Their approach has had mediocre success at best and at worst has caused harm, confusion, and frustration to those receiving the "find what is wrong and fix it" approach. Though this approach has its roots in the science of psychology, it builds on an old and unsuccessful approach. This approach denies the unique design in which we were created and the unique talents which were given to us at birth. Learning about and developing the skills that come from practicing the use of our talents into strengths is the opposite of that old approach.

Stop here for just a minute. Think about this. Does it make more sense to be told and then to study what is wrong with us by focusing on what we aren't good at which leads to negative feelings and thoughts about ourselves? When we focus on our weaknesses using all of the effort we can muster to improve on them, at best we can make them mediocre. Focusing on the weaknesses, we do so at the cost of our attempting to change the way we were created which means we're trying to kill our uniqueness that leads to our being inauthentic. Or, does it make more sense to look for what is right with how we were created by finding out what talents and strengths we've been endowed with and build on what works? Then, once we know what our talents and strengths are, we can begin developing the skills necessary to bring out and develop those talents and strengths. When we focus on our strengths, we can grow exponentially and are not bogged down in being mediocre. And, we are building and growing into our unique and authentic personhood; and we're doing it with an exponential growth factor; in other words, our growth becomes limitless. And just as in our growth being limitless, so does our fulfillment and joy in life.

The psychologists and researchers at Gallup have identified 400 talents which are naturally recurring patterns of thought, feeling, or behavior that can be productively applied. This finding was from a scientific study of over 25,000 people. Further testing found a repetition of these 400 identifiable talents. These talents exist naturally within each of us as predispositions and are not acquired. We're born with them. Each person has a great number of talents which naturally exist within them. These talents are very specific to the individual and are the most real and authentic elements of us. The talents a person has are what makes that person unique. By knowing and applying (developing skills) these unique talents

> ### Talents
>
> *"Talents are naturally recurring patterns of thoughts, feelings, or behavior that can be productively applied."*
> Gallup Strengths Center

for the benefit of others, we demonstrate and revel in what makes us unique. When we look at what makes us unique, think on this, a person's talents work in various combinations (the number of possibilities of combinations is almost unending and unique to each person) each time we apply them to make forward progress for others and ourselves. While we're providing help and value to others, we gain a sense of value, worth, and of being unique. By the way, this is **how** we identify, bring into focus, and develop what today we call our "why."

Our "why"

Viktor Frankl, in his book, *Man's Search for Meaning*, identifies three ways in which we find our "why" by understanding it is through our building of our talents. According to Frankl, we can discover our meaning in life (our why), by 1) creating a work or doing a deed; 2) experiencing something or encountering someone; 3) by the attitude we take toward unavoidable suffering.

We cannot find our "why" by contemplating, pondering, attending seminars, or reading books. By being involved in life, which means being involved in the lives of others, and the attitude we take toward our struggles is how we find our "why." This means we must be engaged in life. To be engaged in life means we must serve others. And the best way in which we can serve others is by knowing our talents, developing them into strengths, and using them. There is no substitute for this.

Additionally, we find our **motivation** within our talents and strengths. By motivation, I am talking about those times in which we get discouraged or depressed. These times are inevitable for us to encounter, but through knowing and applying our talents, we have tools to overcome discouragement.

A talent represents a capacity to do something. This capacity to do something speaks directly to the connection between our talents and our achievements. Our talents are what empower us to hit our goals, move to higher levels of excellence, and fulfill our potential. Remember, talents are naturally recurring patterns of thought, feelings, or behavior which can be productively applied. This means that our talents are automatic, innate, and natural to us and they help us repeatedly do things well. This is why I stress the need for us to **get into our comfort zones** through knowing and developing skills by applying our talents on a daily basis.

Most of us live outside of our talent comfort zone. We don't do this intentionally. Talents

We need to get into our comfort zone; not out of it…we're already out of our comfort zone

are so natural to us we take them for granted, as a matter of fact. More often than not we discount their value because they are so easily applied in our lives. This is why when people compliment us on how well we do something we have a tendency to downplay our effort because to us it has come so easily. It is because of this effortless ability to do certain things well, yet we've not achieved success that we look to others and their tools and methods to achieve our desired success. We try to apply and/or emulate what caused them to be successful and don't realize they may be using their talents and strengths which we can't apply or emulate because their talents and strengths are unique to them.

Therefore, when we attend seminars, meetings, conferences, read books, or listen to podcasts where we are told to get out of our comfort zones to achieve success, we jump at what is being said; we're looking for something that is more difficult, for something that is outside of what we've been doing. Besides, if we could only become just like the speaker or writer, maybe we could have their kind of success. What we haven't considered is that the reason these speakers and writers are so successful is because they are in their comfort zones of talent. Where they fail is in their telling us to become more like them. Then we fail because our attempting to be more like them means our denying our own unique talents we were given at birth. Through the study of our unique set of talents, the practicing of our talents, and the developing skills from the application of using our talents, we are moving ourselves into our comfort zone; **our talent comfort zone**. This becomes the greatest of value to us. The value of our talents isn't to merely help us achieve success, but to take us to levels of excellence, making us exceptional, and exhibiting our unique personhood just as we were created to have and to enjoy.

Talents, when combined to achieve a task, perform a function, accomplish a goal, and any other type of performance necessary for success are called Strengths. A Strength is the ability to consistently provide a near-perfect performance in a specific activity. Strengths are the result of a combination of talent, knowledge, and skill, all working together in concert to produce repeated excellence in a given task. There are several key understandings which can help identify the difference between a talent and a strength.

> *Strengths*
>
> *"A strength is the ability to consistently provide a near-perfect performance in a specific activity."* Gallup
> Strengths Center

1. Talent is what we are born with; a strength is developed by our using our talents (two or more talents) to accomplish a task or project.

2. Talents are natural to us; strengths occur when we apply our talents and develop skills through the application of our talents.

3. Developing skills through our talents is different from developing learned skills outside of the use of our talents and strengths.

4. All of us need to develop skills to accomplish our work. However, we need to be able to identify the

difference between a skill built on talents and a skill built outside of our talents.

5. When we use our talents to develop skills, we naturally, authentically, and effectively help others move forward and make progress.

6. When we apply skills and techniques outside of our talents by attempting to implement another person's talents, it feels manipulative, phony, and inauthentic to those whom we wish to help. Also, it feels the same way to us.

A simple formula to remember (as developed by Donald Clifton) regarding strengths is:

Talent x Knowledge x Skill = Strength

In order to better understand and explain what these talents are and how they are being applied, the psychologists and researchers at Gallup have classified these strengths as Strength Themes.

Strength Themes are the combination of similar talents clustered together. The Gallup organization has created the Gallup Clifton StrengthsFinder assessment tool which identifies 34 clusters of talents that form

> Strength Themes
> *The classifying of what and how talents and strengths are applied*

signature themes in individuals. Each person has his/her own unique strength themes. These 34 Strength Themes are divided into four Domains.

Domains are the result of a natural clustering of how the Strength Themes best work with other people and their strengths in order to develop the most successful teams. The titles for the four Domains have evolved over time to become what they are labeled and how they are defined today. This labeling and defining was arrived at through a statistical factor analysis and a clinical evaluation by Gallup's top scientists. Today, the four Domains are: Executing, Influencing, Relationship Building, and Strategic Thinking. The categorizing of the Strength Themes into Domains provides us with a talent and strength language in which we can better identify, communicate, and celebrate the uniqueness of each of us.

> **Domains**
>
> *Domains are the result of a natural clustering of how the themes best work*

For many years, I observed people in their work and interaction with others with the purpose of identifying their talents. I had become convinced by listening to Dr. Clifton, both in person and on one of his cassette tapes, that if I could identify a person's strengths and create an environment or work atmosphere where they

> *"A person can only perform from strengths. One cannot build performance on weakness, let alone on something one cannot do at all."*
> Peter Drucker

could apply their talents, then, together, we'd be able to achieve greater success for each other and the company for which we worked. However, probably the greatest drawback during this time was my not having a way to easily identify and then communicate with others what their strengths were and how they could best be used. I didn't have a set of words, terms, or concepts of what a person's strengths were so I couldn't clearly, directly, and simply share with them what I perceived their strengths to be and how we might best use them. I had to wing it. With each person I worked, I searched for a word or words that would best help me describe and categorize what I thought might be their talent(s) and then built a job description around those talents. Having to do this for each person was frustrating, painfully slow, and not very efficient and admittedly was certainly not scientific. Because Gallup scientifically identified **400 talents**, classified how these talents could be applied into 34 Strength Themes, and then clustered these Strength Themes into Domains, I now have communication tools which can easily be taught, trained, and transferred to others.

In any training setting, if the training tools and methods employed by the trainer are focused on the personality and strengths of the trainer, then the trainee must have the same or similar personality, style, and talents and strengths as the trainer in order to succeed. If the trainee doesn't have the same strengths as the leader, then the trainee is effectively being told to work on weakness and turn them into strengths in order to be similar to or the same as the trainer. Studies and research has never been able to prove this method to be effective. Rather, these studies and research papers have proven that method to have severely limited effectiveness and more often to have been harmful to the growth of trainees.

Through research and testing, Gallup has found that when ranking a person's strengths from 1 to 34, for any two people to have the same top five strengths is a one out of 278,000-statistical probability.

> *1 out of 278,000 people have the same Top 5 strengths in **any order***

Additionally, for any two people to have the same top five strengths in the same order is a one out of 33,000,000-statistical probability. So, to attempt to make others just like us, we have to abandon the concept that we are uniquely created, have a unique place in this world, and have unique strengths. The insistence of leaders and trainers telling others that their training program must be employed exactly in the same words, manner, and timing of delivery opens the door to a very different formula. It's a formula for destroying people and their uniqueness.

> *1 out of 33,000,000 people have the same Top 5 strengths in the **same order***

In 1986, I purchased a cassette tape on which Dr. Donald O. Clifton shared a formula for destroying people. This is how he said we could accomplish

> **<u>Formula for destroying a person</u>**
> *"Repeatedly tell a person to do something for which s/he has no response in her/his repertoire by which to perform the task."* Dr. Donald O. Clifton

the destruction of people, "repeatedly tell a person to do something for which s/he had no response in her/his repertoire by which to perform the task." Instead of providing an environment for their trainees or their downline to grow and develop as leaders, this training by duplication produces leaners who are constantly needing to be propped up, pushed, and enticed into doing what the leader needs to have happen for their own success. We don't need more leaners!

In order for leaders to develop and grow, trainees need to be trained by focusing on their talents and their capacity to develop their strengths in areas where they can produce a near perfect performance. This means taking the time to identify what each of our people is good at, finding the right tools to help them become successful, and then training them on the use of those tools. If you think this sounds hard, possibly even more difficult than anything you've ever done, you're probably right. Focusing on people rather than things will be the hardest work you'll have ever done or ever will do. But, the rewards will be the greatest for yourself, and for them.

Every person has the capacity to be a leader. However, in order for people to grow into being leaders, they must have the capacity for a near perfect performance in order to excel and succeed. Finding each person's capacity to excel through a near perfect performance is called finding their talent. The combination of these talents working together is called strengths and it is

> *EVERY PERSON has the capacity to be a leader*

through these strengths which we effortlessly perform every day that we each have the capacity to become leaders.

Toward the end of a coaching session, I asked the person I was coaching what strengths she thought would be the most successful in leadership. She immediately identified strengths other than her own. Her perception was that there are certain types of people who could become leaders and she wasn't one of them. As we talked further about this, I asked her about a couple of people whom I thought most people would consider leaders and she too thought of them as leaders. I asked her what she thought their style was and what they might have for strengths. Again, she identified both style and strengths other than her own. When I shared with her that they actually had the exact same style and similar strengths as she, she was speechless. But the point had been made and as we talked further, she began to understand that it isn't that there is a certain style or a certain set of strengths that make people successful. I explained to her that the success that people have is based on their performing in a capacity to build on their strengths instead of their weaknesses.

I've found that for most people, because our strengths are effortless on our part, we consider our strengths to be an everyday occurrence for everybody. But, to those whose lives have been positively affected by those with strengths different from their own, it is evident that their strengths are significant, not every day ho-hum like our own, but

> *Our talents and strengths are effortless to us, because they are ours*

significant, possibly bordering on the heroic. Through the identifying and then focusing on the strengths of people, we build leaders not leaners. We unleash that near perfect performance inside of others and we see the brilliance they bring to and naturally share with those around them. Are training tools and methods employed? Absolutely! However, the focus is on people and the strengths of the individuals, not the program or the method. Does this take more time? Sure. It is always easier to manage things than it is to lead by building on specific strengths of people, but the results of leading people based on their specific strengths far out-performs and outweighs the management of things over time…everytime.

What about Weaknesses?

At the end of a coaching session with one of our teammates, during which our discussion was centered on her strengths, I was taken aback. She looked at me and, with a clear look that said she had a suspicion of charlatanism on my part, asked, "Ok, if these are my strengths, what are my weaknesses? You can't always just talk about your strengths without knowing what your weaknesses are. If you do this, then how do you ever grow? And if you don't talk about your weaknesses, then isn't this just a scam or a hoax to get people to buy into your program?"

I asked her if she knew what her weaknesses were. She said she did but was hoping that I would identify her weaknesses through some program to see if they matched and if so was there some "magic" I could share with her to help her overcome them. I said, "If you'll tell me what your weaknesses are, we'll talk through them one by one and I'll show you how you can overcome them or make them irrelevant by focusing on your strengths." I went on to explain that there are basically two ways I can work with people in helping them to overcome their weaknesses.

The first is to focus on their strengths and practice using them to overcome the perceived weakness.

A second way is to look to others who have strengths in her area of weakness and see if they can team up with help her overcome the weakness. Either way, the goal is to focus on the strength; not the weakness. We need

> "The task of leadership is to create an alignment of strengths, making our weaknesses irrelevant." Peter Drucker

others to achieve thing even greater than we can achieve by our ourselves, and this means and encourages teamwork. Teams working together in areas where near perfect performances occur naturally produces extraordinary results.

However, there is a pervasive theory regarding strengths and weaknesses which continues to be taught and, in my opinion, is damaging to the building of a person's strengths. This theory is that if we focus on our strengths they will become too strong and will hurt others. Wrong! It isn't that our strengths become too strong. It is that we haven't developed the maturity of the talent and/or strength to practice the versatility of working with others. This is where the concept and application of the SOCIAL STYLE MODEL™® of Versatility is so practical and helpful.

Remember, **"a strength is the ability to consistently provide a near-perfect performance in a specific activity."**

This means that when I am using my strengths, I am doing something good. I'm benefiting others with my God-given talents and strengths for their betterment. To me this seems like a good thing, something which should make me glad and cause me to feel good inside. Yet, there are times when we have used our strengths and the results were less than "near perfect." Instead of succeeding in helping the person or group of people, we created friction and frustration. They went away complaining that we were, "pushy," or "arrogant," or "proud," or "controlling" or some other negatively descriptive word or words. When hearing this, we came away feeling critical of them, not wanting to help again, and looking for a way out to get away from these ungrateful yahoos, so we can lick our wounds. This is when we're told that our strengths are too strong, that our strength has actually become a weakness in our life, or that we need to tone down a particular strength because it has hurt others. And, for the most part we go along with this thinking because it is obvious to everyone that our need to perform our strength is the perpetrator of this pain. Therefore, our strength is too strong, and it has become a weakness. Doesn't everyone agree with this? Wouldn't you agree with this? I mean, this has happened to all of us from time to time, so it must be that our strength is a weakness, right?

Let me state again…Wrong! Let's dissect what actually

took place. I used my strength, accomplished a near-perfect performance, meaning that through the use of my strengths a nearly perfect result was achieved for the betterment of others or the group. However, when I did achieve, and maybe even surpassed, the desired results, I also ticked off some folks who didn't like the way I executed my near-perfect performance. Was it the strength that was the weakness? The **use** of my strength achieved the correct result but the **way** I used my strength was distasteful, possibly abrasive to those whom I was attempting to benefit. It wasn't the **result** of my strength, but it was my **behavioral application** of the strength that caused the conflict. In other words, I offended people by my behavior not my strength. This behavioral application is called Versatility, and this example shows a lack of Versatility. The behavioral application of Versatility is found and taught through the SOCIAL STYLE MODEL™®.

However, before moving on to the topic of Versatility, a couple more thoughts regarding weaknesses are needed.

First, a correct definition of weakness is **"anything which hinders us from making progress or the team which we are part of making progress toward the desired goal/success."**

Second, there are three significant contributing factors to any one or more of our strengths becoming a weakness.

- The first is illness. When we aren't feeling well due to minor illnesses, such as a cold or the flu, we need to get away from others and find a comfortable place where we can recuperate. The work will be there when we are well again. God wants us, His children, to get their proper (let me emphasize this word again, *proper* rest and He wants us to take care of ourselves when we become ill.

- The second is if we are over-tired. Too often in the world in which most people live today, we push ourselves to the point of exceeding our physical capability. We need rest! We need sleep! We weren't made to work all day, party all night, and expect to perform at our best the following day. This is where the phrase often found on T-shirts is most applicable, "Sometimes I wake up grumpy, other times I let him sleep!"

- And the third is stressed out. When we're stressed out in our relationships, family, work, or whatever, we are the most vulnerable to misusing or misapplying our talents and strengths.

Versatility

Versatility is a measurement of a person's ability to meet people in a manner in which others are receptive to receiving information. A person with low Versatility displays poor Style Awareness, possibly their own and more likely others, and is focused on meeting their own needs. A person with high Versatility is aware of their own Style, focuses on other person's Style, yet effectively stays in their own Style. The greater the Versatility, the greater the success for all people. Versatility is introduced in the chapter titled, "Relationships: Foundations for Success." By perfecting our ability to apply Versatility, we enhance our Strengths by not offending others during the execution of our Strengths.

In order to bring out the best in our strengths we must use our strengths for the benefit of others. It's not enough to know what our strengths are; we must give them away. It is only in the using of our strengths for the benefit of others that we are able to experience the value our strengths bring to the world. Actually, when we use our strengths we can get emotionally high (energized) out of being able to express or engage our talents. It makes us feel there is a place for us in this world. By giving our strengths away, we receive the great gift of seeing value in our lives, experiencing our worth through our benefiting the lives of others and this world, creating hope, and clarifying a vision for our lives by dreaming of what we might become and do. We know, that is with our mind and we feel with our heart that we are vital to ourselves and others. We become motivated to be more and to do more. The key to our being motivated lies within us. Motivation is found in our talents and strengths. This is called intrinsic motivation. Only intrinsic motivation continues to motivate us beyond the difficulties encountered while we're pursuing our goals. Additionally, this giving away of our strengths for the benefit of others is a foundational element to our knowing and understanding our "Why."

8
Sharing – Consultative Sales

> ***Sharon Daniels***
> President and CEO AchieveGlobal (retired);
> Executive/Senior Leader – Providing Interim
> Management, Project, and Consulting Role
>
> *Many, if not most, organizations now view consultative selling as the baseline, regardless of their industry, geography or customer base. Salespeople who succeed at developing these relationships do so by continuously understanding customer needs, and by providing solutions that help customers reach their goals.*

There are two types of methods or ways people approach sales: transactional or consultative.

1. Transactional sales is about selling or getting people to buy a product.
2. Consultative sales is about listening to the prospect, and then as the consultant is listening to what prospects are saying, the consultant identifies the needs of the prospect.

Of these two types of sales approaches, the more successful method of sales is Consultative Sales.

Many times the prospect isn't even aware of their needs and it's the person listening, the consultant, who identifies and points out what the prospect is looking for by posing the right questions and interpreting the answers. There is a lot of give and take between the prospect and the consultant while the consultant continues to clarify what the prospect's needs might be. This is called having a discussion. It's an opening dialogue with another person in order for the consultant to be of help without jumping at solving a problem by selling a product. Sometimes during this discussion, the consultant can help the prospect resolve their need without purchasing a product because they already have the solution(s) to their problem and don't need to buy.

If you've made it this far after having read the word "sales" in the chapter title and having it repeated several times in the first paragraph, without throwing up or dropping the book into the nearest recycling bin, congratulations. At the heart of what we do in dōTERRA® is to "share" with others the wonderful results dōTERRA®'s essential oils can provide for everyone. This is actually called sales. If you believe

> *Sales is not a **four-letter word**. The misuse of sales is what is objectionable and leads many to use **four-letter words**.*

that what we are doing is building a movement of people, both Wholesale Customers and Wellness Advocate Builders, the only way is for us to "share" with others; this, is called sales. If you believe that this movement of people can and is having a positive impact on the health care world, all around the globe, then you have to agree that someone, somewhere is "sharing" with those who have not yet heard; this is called sales. Embrace the term!

Throughout this chapter, I'm going to be using the word "sales." To me, the word sales and the process of sales is not derogatory or problematic. In fact, having studied professional sales, known as Consultative Sales, for over 35 years, I've found that when the process of Consultative Sales is properly understood and applied, both the prospect and the sales person come away from the transaction feeling good about what they just did and about themselves. The prospect has had someone listen to them, maybe for the first time in a very long time, and that person has come alongside and helped the prospect solve a need. The sales person has been able to use their talents and strengths to help another person make progress toward their goal and has gained a new friend. This is as "sales" should occur. Unfortunately in a sales situation for most of us, we've had everything but this happen more often than we'd like to remember. As you read this chapter on Consultative Sales, take the time to reflect on the science behind the process of sales and then ponder the art of using this process to help others. It is in the serving of others where we find the greatest expression of who we are. Consulting with people to help define their need and find a solution is extremely rewarding for both parties.

Continuing now with a discussion on Transactional Sales and Consultative Sales, to better understand the differences in these processes there needs to be a brief explanation of what each of these approaches is and how each functions.

Transactional Sales

Transactional Sales is a product sale whereby the sales person is focused on getting their product into the hands and homes of customers. There is little or no customer service except when necessary. The focus is on the selling of the product. This type of sale is great for those customers who believe they know which product they want and are looking for the least expensive and easiest method of getting it. This type of sales generally appeals to less than 25% of the population. Sometimes this type of selling method is referred to as product sales.

Most sales people don't want to admit they are product salespeople. However, the reality is that most sales people are transactional salespeople. Authors of popular self-help sales books will often disguise their transactional sales approach by phrasing their wording to make it sound like they are really helping people buy. They will use phrases like, "helping people want to buy what you're selling." On the surface this sounds really good, but when you scratch away the veneer you'll find they're still using the transactional approach of selling a product, not serving a need of the client.

> *Transactional Sales focuses on the product, not the needs of the prospect*

There is a place for transactional sales. Most retail stores are transactional sales where the customer can get easy access to the product, make a quick purchase, and get out with the product. Most direct sales and MLM sales are transactional sales. The reason for this is it is easier to learn about a product's features and benefits, focus the customer's attention on what their product will do for the customer by identifying those features and benefits, and then "help" the prospect buy the products.

Some of the more significant problems with using a transactional sales approach are:

- focus is on the product not the customer
- sales person operates more like an order taker
- continually needs to feed a pipeline with the names of new people to get them to buy
- sees customers as a means to satisfy the sales person's goals
- sale is on price and being competitive; little or no customer loyalty

In summary, Transactional Sales does have a place in the marketplace, but that place is not in a business where there needs to be a relationship developed between the customer and the sales person. Additionally, where there is a need to develop and use team concepts and efforts, Transactional Sales misses the mark of people as more important than things. When the value of the sales person is necessary for the betterment of the customer a different sales approach and process needs to occur. In dōTERRA®, we have such a unique product in its market, education and a trusting relationship are necessary. Consultative Sales is a distinctive and marked departure from Transactional Sales.

Consultative Sales

Consultative Sales is focused on the needs of the prospect and the sales person becomes the consultant to the prospect. The sales person asks questions to determine the prospect's needs and then using this information offers a solution or solutions for those needs. A key word here is consultant. Let me say this again, the sales person becomes a consultant to the prospect. By being the expert in both knowledge of the products and in having an ability to connect the prospect's needs with the products, the salesperson establishes him/herself as a consultant. In order for this to occur there needs to be a change in the mindset of the salesperson. This shift in mindset means the salesperson has to position him/herself as an expert in his/her field and as one who is offering advice to the prospect on how his/her products will help the prospect. This shift in mindset is extremely important. There are two chapters in this book where I talk about building relationships with others and building on our and other's talents and strengths. Both of these tools are key foundational values which are instrumental in gaining this shift in mindset to become a consultant to the prospect.

> *Consultative Sales focuses on the needs of the people, applying products to solve their needs*

In order for people to become consultants, they need to learn the Consultative Sales Process. This Process consists of seven (7) stages the consultant takes a prospect through in order to better serve the needs of the prospect.

Knowing these seven stages helps the consultant know where they are in any stage of the process while working with the prospect. Knowing these seven stages helps the consultant stay focused on where s/he is in the conversational sales process with the prospect. Knowing these seven stages is the science behind the sales process. Consultative selling is a **two-way** conversation; it's not a monologue; it's not scripted. It is not a manipulation of the prospect and there aren't any schematics that hinge on the next steps of what to do if the prospect says "yes" the salesperson says one thing and if the prospect says "no" then the salesperson says another thing. Consultative Sales is not following the schematic to box the prospect into agreeing to buy. Consultative selling is real, open, honest and transparent; in another word, authentic. Consultative Sales is a conversation/consultation with a prospect about his/her challenges, goals, objectives and how the salesperson can help him/her resolve these issues through helpful service and correct products.

> *Consultative sales is a two-way conversation – **SHARING**; not a monologue*

By knowing and applying the 7 stages in the Consultative Sales process of working with others, you'll find that 95% of selling is in the first 5 stages and that only 5% of what we do to help others is in the 6th stage. This is the stage that frightens most people - closing. The 7th stage is when the building of individuals begins, not ends. This 7th stage is often overlooked by calling it "follow-up".

9
Consultative Sales...Helping Others

Just because there are 7 stages in the Consultative Sales Process you don't have to follow each stage in a sequential or progressive order. This means you could start with a benefit to the prospect and not even get into the features of the product. By using the Consultative Sales Process, you listen to what the prospect needs help with and you start there. Knowing the behavioral style of the person with whom you're sharing is vital to knowing which stage is best suited to their learning preference. You might find yourself talking to someone who is analytical in how they prefer to be treated and how they prefer to receive information. If this is the case, you might begin by talking about the features of the product or the company. But, if you do this, even though the person is analytical s/he will still be looking for the benefit of the product, so don't get bogged down in the details of the features. Highlight the features and look for openings to move to the benefits as quickly as possible.

You might have heard there is an art and a science to sales. This is one of those absolutely true statements of the Consultative Sales Process. The Consultative Sales process defines and explains the science behind the Process and at the same time it provides the latitude necessary for the art of the sale. Only knowing and using the science, the facts, and data of your product will leave your prospect well informed but it won't compel them to do something about what they've learned. It is in the art of the sale where you combine the knowledge of what you know about the product with the value it'll bring to the prospect and then it will all come together for the prospect to act on the information you've provided by purchasing the product(s) and/or becoming a Wellness Advocate or a Wholesale Customer. It is through the science of knowing and then knowing that you know, that the art can then paint the picture for the prospect of how to change, improve, or better their lives. Learning the science of the process is vital to anyone's success. However, if we stop with the science and we don't move to the art of the process, we will never be able to be of service to others, helping them with their needs. The art of what we do is what makes what we do look easy. The art of the process connects the human and emotional values of the prospect to the product, and that empowers the prospect to change and to grow.

Many times I've been put on the spot by a client, a donor, or a co-worker looking to me to find a solution to a problem they're working through. Several years ago, I was having lunch with a development officer of a major university for which we both worked, and one of her donor prospects. During lunch, the development officer praised the donor for his generosity to the college she represented and thanked him over and over for his kindness. She was and is very good at what she does. The donor was so overwhelmed with her praise and thankfulness that he said he was ready to make another gift to her college and he wanted to create another life insurance policy on two of his grandchildren, giving the ownership of the policy and proceeds at the time of their deaths to the college. Both the development officer and the donor were having an exciting time talking about how wonderful and valuable this would be to the college. Shortly, the development officer turned to me and asked what the steps were for the donor to do this. Since the donor had said he wanted to place the policy on the lives of the two grandchildren, my concern was how young the grandchildren were at that time. By knowing the features of the insurance companies' (plural because we worked with a large number of them) guidelines on insurability and the university's policy on their minimum age of an insured in order for us to accept a policy, I was concerned there might be a problem. So, I asked the donor, "How old are your grandchildren?" His reply was, "Jamie is 16 and Andrew is 14." Looking at the development officer, I could tell she knew there was a problem. She knew the age requirements necessary for the university to accept an insurance policy.

It was my responsibility to let the donor know that because of his grandchildren's young ages that we wouldn't be able to accept any life insurance policies on his grandchildren. He was heartbroken. He said he had hoped he could increase his giving for the current year by leveraging (he knew this feature because both the development officer and I had educated him on

> *I'll give you until you finish chewing your food to come up with an answer!"*

this) an amount of current funds he'd set aside to a larger, deferred gift so he could qualify for a specific level of giving within the college. Looking at him, then at the development officer, I was feeling the pain of what I had to do next. I had to explain that we couldn't use a life insurance gift because of the ages of his grandchildren. Once I explained this, my thought was that we would all have to just accept the fact that we couldn't help the donor with his wishes at that time. So, I looked down at my plate and chose to eat another bite of food. Just after I began chewing the food, the development officer looked at me and said, "George, I know you're not going to let my donor down by telling him there isn't any way he can give my college a gift this year. I know you have something up your sleeve and that you can make my donor happy. Now, what is it? I'll give you until you finish chewing your food to come up with an answer!"

Remember, this was at lunch. When I heard this I wondered if I could keep chewing until the restaurant closed and that by then they'd forget about what I'd just been challenged to do. But, knowing that development officer, I knew she wasn't going to let me off the hook that easy. I had 24 of the recommended 27 minimum chews of my food left before I had to come up with something.

In my mind I was racing through a matrix of features and benefits of planned gift products, insurance policies, and the university gift acceptance policies. When I was at about chew number 12, there was a tumbler click in the features, advantages, and benefits matrix of my mind. I'd hit on something! It just might work! Slowly, putting my fork down and picking up my pen, I opened up my notebook. There was as much anticipation on the faces of the donor and the development officer as there was in my mind. I was still churning through a solution by using the features and benefits along with the policies and restrictions to provide a possible answer to their concerns and questions.

As I worked through this solution in my mind, I also began to write out the possible answer on the paper in my notebook. Their eyes were glued to the paper, as they were expectantly listening to every word I said. I laid the solution out for them to consider and after a few questions as to how this could play out in the real world (not just my head), we all came to the same conclusion. This could work! And not only did it work, we offered this opportunity to a number of other donors who, prior to this time, had been told there wasn't a way around this same problem. Several millions of dollars were raised for the benefit of a number of schools and colleges within the university, many more donors were thrilled to be able to increase their deferred and current giving, new relationships between older alums and younger alums were forged due to this newly designed opportunity, loyalty to the schools and colleges deepened, and development officers were able to become heroes in the eyes of their donors and schools or colleges. All of this because of my knowing the 7 stages of the Consultative Sales Process. **I knew the science.** And because of my skill in using the SOCIAL STYLE® Model in helping others, **I knew the art.** We provided the product that the prospect (a donor, in this case) needed in a consultative sales victory. The process worked in this case, and it will work in cases for dōTERRA® and other ventures as well.

10
The Consultative Sales Process

Stage 1 – Product Knowledge

Knowing your products for most of us working with dōTERRA® essential oils is probably the easiest part of this whole process. We love the oils and we love to share with others about the oils. I remember when Norma first learned about the oils, she came home and couldn't wait for me to talk with her about having attended a meeting where the subject was health and wellness and that there were products available to help people use natural means to achieve this. She enrolled that same night, and from that day forward, day and night she would pour over what each of the oils is, how it can be helpful to our bodies, how they are all natural and from God, and how they can help people bring a balance of health to their lives. She learned the products!

However, for us to become great at knowing how the oils can be of value to those whom we serve, we need to know the product and then be able to communicate about what we know to others. What is needed is for us to know the features and the benefits of each oil and of dōTERRA®. We need to be able to talk about the advantages, especially now, with the scrutiny of the FDA helping all of us become not just compliant but to become professional in our knowledge and communication of the effectiveness of the oils. We need to be able to accurately, clearly, and effectively communicate what the oils are capable of doing, why we have chosen to use dōTERRA® oils, and what our role is in helping to change the world in how people view and work out their own health. Most of the time we see and communicate with others as we see things. However, we need to be able to link the features of our products to the benefits they provide because not all people can easily do this. Therefore, we need to know the **features**, the **advantages**, and the **benefits** of the company we have chosen to use as our wholesaler of essential oils and the **features**, the **advantages**, and the **benefits** of each of these oils and products.

> *Have to know our products in order to serve the needs of others*

Here is something for you to consider: If the stated difficulty with a number of people you are inviting to join is due to the price of the oils or the cost to become a Wholesale Customer or a Wellness Advocate Builder, then you are probably doing a less than adequate job in communicating the features, the advantages, and the benefits of dōTERRA® and dōTERRA®'s essential oils.

Features

A product feature is a physical characteristic, or a description of the product itself. The features of the product identify **what it is**. We must be able to do this objectively; that is, without placing a judgment value or an opinion on the company or product. I know, how in the world can we do this when we are so excited about the value dōTERRA® and their oils bring to the world?! However, if we are going to be able to effectively and clearly communicate to others what we know, then we must learn how to do this in an objective and empirical manner. This is "the crawling before the walking" part of this stage. Identifying features will give us the foundation of what the company and/or product is.

Features cover such things as identifying the ingredients of products, the unique attributes of the company, what each product can do, product specifications which are detailed descriptions of requirements, dimensions, materials used, etc. Keep in mind that features do not help the person to buy or you to sell. It is <u>important and necessary</u> for you to know what the features of the oils are so you'll be able to define the product's value to the prospect (the advantage), and identify for the prospect the emotional value and reasoning for their using the product (benefit).

Advantages

Advantages are like the intermediary between features and benefits; they are effectively **what the feature does** to eventually result in a benefit. Advantages provide the bridge between what a product is and what the product means to a prospect. Knowing what the advantage of the product is gives us the ability to help the prospect connect the dots between the features and the benefits. Using the knowledge of what the advantage of a product is provides the prospect with the logical progression from what the product does to how the prospect is helped by the product.

Benefits

The biggest difference between a feature and a benefit is that the benefit affects the emotional level and values of the prospect. This is where the prospect relates to the product. This is where the prospect can feel, not just reason, the value of the product for their own, personal needs. Benefits of products paint pictures in the hearts and emotions of the prospect. Benefits allow the prospect to have what is called "aha", moments where they can see what the product can do for them. This is where features are transformed into advantages and benefits. If we only talk about the features of the products and not the advantages and benefits, we run the risk of the prospect drawing their own conclusions and they may not be the correct ones. It is our responsibility to be knowledgeable of the oils to the point where we help the prospect connect the dots for their own use. And, it is our responsibility to do this in a way that is both rationally and emotionally appealing to the prospect.

> *The "aha" moments are the moments of self-discovery. True learning only occurs when self-discovery bursts on the scene.*

Understanding and applying the benefits of a product to the needs of the prospect is likened to the selling of a steak;

sell the sizzle, not the steak. Don't just factually describe the steak, paint the picture of a sizzling steak. Think about this; steak, fresh off the grill, still popping and hissing from the heat, as it's placed in front of you with your knife in one hand and your fork in the other, the savory aroma tantalizing your nose as your taste buds anticipate the first bite. Are you salivating yet? This is delivering the value of the benefit of a product to the prospect so that the prospect can visualize and actualize its value to them and their family. Here is where it will also be helpful to know if your prospect is vegan! And here is where it is vital to have observed the behavioral style of that prospect so you can speak and act to their style.

Also, when you are talking to the prospect about the benefits of the product, share some stories that apply to your conversation. People would much rather listen to a story they can relate to than hear facts (features) of the product. If you don't know how to tell a story, then listen to some storytellers, join Toastmasters International or some other organization which offers you an opportunity to learn about and practice storytelling. It is my belief that everyone, without exception, has stories they can tell. It is also my belief that the reason more people don't tell stories is they don't believe they can. It is not a matter of not having stories to tell, it is a matter of not believing your stories are worth telling. If this is the case, then take time to read and learn more about Talents and Strengths found in this book and on the internet. Take the Strengths test and when you get your results, read them every week for 7

> *People like to hear stories that relate to the subject...learn to tell stories*

weeks and you'll find you have some amazing strengths. From knowing what your strengths are and how you've been able to apply these strengths to help others, you'll be re-living what happened and you'll be telling yourself a story. Now, go out and begin telling others your stories; don't worry if you're not polished in the presentation, just begin practicing.

I love to tell stories, but it wasn't always true of my life. I had to think who a couple of great storytellers were, look for a way to emulate what they did, yet keep it within my range of experiences, and I practiced. I practiced on every client I met and I practiced telling stories to my friends. After doing this for several years, I joined Toastmasters, International, and was given opportunities to broaden my storytelling. I have practiced to the point that now, when I'm about to launch into a story, if Norma is in the group, she'll politely excuse herself by saying that if she stayed to hear my story it would be the 467th time. In fairness to Norma, her Pop and I would tell stories, many times the same story many times over. One day the two of us were seated in the kitchen of his house and from noon until about 8:30 that night we told each other stories. Norma would come and go and from time to time she'd ask the same question, "Didn't you guys already tell that story?" Pop's answer was classic! His response was, "Well, I believe we did. But you see, it's not really the story that we're interested in. It's the tellin' of the story and it's the tellin' that is important." So, practice your storytelling.

Homework

On a sheet of paper or in your computer, create a matrix with Products, Features, Advantages, and Benefits written across the top of the page. Draw a line under each of the four of these. Divide each of these four into a separate column by drawing vertical lines. Products should be your first column, Features in the second, Advantages in the third, and Benefits in the fourth. Place the names of each of the oils under the Product column. Give yourself enough line space to write out three or more features, advantages, and benefits for each oil. Through practicing this you'll gain a clearer understanding and also a better working knowledge of the products, what they do, and how they will benefit those with whom you share. The Product Information Pages or the Approved Claims List are helpful in this assignment. Both are found on deterra.com.

The following are some samples of how features, benefits, and advantages can be applied to dōTERRA®'s handling of the essential oils they offer and the makeup of dōTERRA®, the company. I've left the work of identifying the features, benefits, and advantages of dōTERRA®, the company, to you. You can find the information you'll need to do this exercise on dōTERRA®'s website.

Let me encourage you again, take the time to review the samples I've provided. Add your own research on dōTERRA®'s vision, mission, processing of essential oils, and company to what I've provided. Get to know dōTERRA®'s products by identifying their features, benefits, and advantages. This is the foundational stage upon which you need to build.

Quality and Potency of dōTERRA®'s Essential Oils

Distillation

Feature: steam or cold pressed or expressed for highest potency for each oil

Advantage: proper distillation to ensure the highest consistency of the oil's chemistry from beginning to its bottled use

Benefit: confident they will consistently work for the intended purpose

Oil Sourcing

Feature: using plants from their indigenous environment offers the highest potency for therapeutic use

Advantage: gathering the oils from plants and trees grown in their indigenous environment promotes the best profile of aromatic compounds

Benefits: users of the oils can be confident the oils will do what is expected of them consistently.

dōTERRA®

<u>Vision</u>

Feature: science company that builds people

Advantage: focus is on people not products

Benefit: fastest growing company in US history to reach billion in sales

<u>Business Structure</u>

Feature: inverted MLM income structure

Advantage: promotes the value of building people, longevity in business, serving others

Benefits: people can see and feel there is a corporate concern for the well-being of those who experience promoting and using dōTERRA®'s essential oils. People feel loved

11
The Consultative Sales Process

Stage 2 – Prospects

Sitting across the desk from my agency manager in my new job as an insurance agent, I asked him, "So how do I start? Who do I talk to first? And what should I say to them?"

His reply was, "Anybody that you see is who you should talk to, and ask them if they want to buy life insurance."

I looked at him and thought to myself that his advice seemed pretty vague. I know that if someone were to come up to me, a person I'd never met, to ask me if I wanted to buy life insurance, I'd probably say, "No, not interested. Get away from me, and, what kind of a nut are you?" But needing to do well in that new venture and needing to provide for my family, instead of saying what I really thought, I looked at him and asked this question, "How many people do you think I should see in a week and ask them that question?"

"In order to be successful in this business you need to talk to 40 new people every single week!"

And that ended the extent of my training from my agency manager as I entered what would become my career for the next 15 years as an insurance agent, financial planner, and estate planner and another 25 years in working with charitable organizations as a planned gift specialist. I probably should have guessed I wouldn't get a very satisfying or helpful response to my question regarding who I should talk to about insurance because of his answer to a previous question a couple of weeks prior to this conversation.

I had asked him for training shortly after I signed on with the insurance company and more specifically with this manager's agency. My question to him at that time was, "When will I receive my training and what will it consist of?" His response was that his secretary was both his assistant and the trainer in our agency and I should arrange an appointment to meet with her to have her go through my training. I arranged a meeting with her at the agency office. When I got there she took me to the manager's office, placed a box that was about 2 feet high and about 3 feet long on his conference table, and she proceeded to train me. My training consisted of her taking a book out of the box, reading the title, and then handing me the book; taking another book out of the box, reading the title, handing the book to me; and reaching for the next book. This went on until the box was half-empty. Recognizing the pain and agony I was experiencing and the feeling of frustration she was having by doing something she was not trained or equipped to do, I looked at her and asked, "How many times have you gone through this with another person in the agency?" Her reply was classic, "You're the first one I've ever done this with and, frankly, I hope I'm doing a good job." Well, having gone through the third grade and having learned how to read, I decided it would be better for both her and me if I took the box of books home and looked through them to see if they would be of any help to me. And that is exactly what I did. And like any good sales trainee when I carried that box of books into my office, I found a nice, comfortable, cozy corner in which to set the box of books, just in case I might need to read them someday. So began my training into the sales process.

When my agency manager said I needed to see 40 people every week and then ask each of them if they would like to buy life insurance, I needed to figure out exactly how long I would have a before I ran out of people to talk to or they ran me out of town. At that time there were approximately 22,000 people living in the county in which I lived and in which I had grown up. Knowing that the statistical average size family was approximately 4.5 people, I took that into consideration when I began my calculations. However, being a bright, young man and knowing there were several families within the county who had 24 or more children, I knew I'd need to make an upward adjustment to 5 people per family. 22,000 people divided by five equals 4,400 prospects. This meant that if I talked to 40 people every week I would have approximately 110 weeks of work before I ran out of names of people to see. Yet, I next factored in that I wanted to have some time and fun with my family, so I allowed 4 weeks for vacations and holidays. Taking 4 weeks away from 52 weeks gave me about 48 weeks of work each year. 110 weeks of prospects divided by 48 weeks per year of work projected that I would run out of prospects to talk with or be run out of town in about two years and 14 weeks. This made absolutely no sense to me. But I was stuck. I needed to make money; I needed to take care of my family; and I needed to pay my bills.

It took five months before I had figured out just about every way that you could fail as a life insurance agent. By then the company stipend had run out and the company had become disillusioned regarding my potential success, as had I, and so they placed me on straight commission. This meant I was facing less than $100 worth of income in the month of November. Christmas was coming! Winter was upon us! This wouldn't cover more than half of my heating bill for one month (this was in Minnesota). I figured I didn't have much choice; I needed to look for another job. But, about that time a friend of mine called and asked if he and I could get together for lunch. I said I'd be glad to as long as he was buying. He said he would buy my lunch, so we got together. Our conversation was the turning point for me and truly the beginning of my 35+ year career in sales and helping people.

Listening to my story of how I had failed, my friend suggested that I should be working with people who knew me or knew of me. He went on to say that since I had grown up as a mink rancher in the area, I should be working with farmers and that I should be working with them on their estate plans. I looked at him and asked him what in the world estate plans were. He briefly explained and once he had finished his explanation I said, "George, I don't know anything about estate plans or estate planning. I wouldn't know the first place to start." (Yes, we are both named George) He said to me," George, you don't have to know anything about estate planning or how to do estate planning. There is an attorney who has worked with our agency for several years who will do all the estate planning and all you've got to do is sell the people the amount of insurance he tells them they need to take care of their tax problems." I sat back in the booth and thought to myself, "Wow, this sounds too easy to be true, but what have I got to lose? I'm not making any money right now and it is a tough time of the year to try to find another job. In fact, it might take me 6-8 weeks or more to go through interviews and get another job and then more time before I'd get paid for the work at this new job." Looking at my friend I said, "Okay, how do I start?" He gave me the name of the attorney, I called him, (this call to the attorney is an amazing, unique, and miraculous conversation in itself and if we ever get to meet in person feel free to ask me about this, I'll be glad to tell you the story), and he agreed to work with me. I contacted the insurance company's home office, found out there were estate planning forms I could fill out while talking to people, and there was an Estate Planning department which would help me create plans for my clients.

What my friend, George, did for me when he told me I should be talking with people whom I either knew or who knew of me was a turning point for me. He opened the door for me to understand what prospecting is, who my prospects were, and what to do with them. This was the beginning of my sales education. Over the years I've learned that most sales people fail because they don't know how to prospect, not because they don't know how to open and close sales meetings. And this isn't just because I've learned this, I've experienced it!. In the sales industry, managers are taught to have all of their new sales people create a list of between 100 and 300 names of people the sales person can call on. Generally, once this is done and the sales person has talked to most or all of the people on their list, they don't know how to resupply their list. This leads to failure. However, this doesn't have to be the case. And especially it doesn't have to be the case in our working with dōTERRA®.

Why start with the names of the people you know? Starting with the people you know and have some type of relationship with is called your warm market. A warm market contains the names of people with whom you have an existing relationship. They could be family members, friends, co-workers (at least the ones you like), and any others whose names are in your phone or email contact list. Generally, these people trust you and they would be willing and interested in hearing what you're doing, whether you'd seen a good movie, shared a love for a special TV show, liked a good restaurant and wanted them to have the same kind of experience, or any other life experience you'd share with them. Gather all of their names and contact information and either keep their names on an excel spreadsheet, a piece of paper which you won't lose, or a calendar… somewhere you can refer to them over the next couple of years. Yes, I'm saying the next couple of years. You're not going to see all of them in the next few weeks or months. If you do, then you're working harder not smarter; you would be working against your relationship with them; you're using wrong thinking toward how to work with your warm market. So, slow down. Take a breath.

If you run out immediately and try to tell everyone on your list that you've just become a Wellness Advocate and now they should also, you'll more than likely end up burning some bridges with your warm market and you'll quickly run out of names. I know in direct sales or network marketing, the training usually centers on duplication, which is addition; I want you to begin thinking in terms of multiplication.

Most people think prospecting is just going out and sharing with anyone or anything that moves. It falls in line with the phrase, "if it moves, shoot it!" Wrong! Proper and successful prospecting lays the groundwork and the foundation for everything that happens throughout the entire time of the Wellness Advocate's career. Prospecting starts with those with whom you have a personal relationship. While you're doing this you look for evidence of the principles of multiplication in the lives of those in both your warm market and those whom you don't yet know, your cold market. Using the principles of multiplication as your roadmap to finding builders, you'll also find those who aren't yet ready to be builders, and you'll find those who don't have any interest in building, but love the oils.

"if it moves, shoot it!"

One last word on prospecting. Put everyone's name on an excel spreadsheet or a piece of paper. Don't worry you won't be calling all of them immediately. Remember, I said earlier you will probably need about one to two years to go through your list. The list is there for a number of reasons. First, it's a place to start. You're going to pick and choose key people with whom you want to connect immediately, so do this. Second, there will come a lull in the building of your team and you'll say to yourself, "Self, you don't have anyone left to talk to. You might just as well pack up your kits, send them back to dōTERRA® and ask for your money back. And if that doesn't work, you might as well put them on ebay and sell them for the highest price." No, don't you dare do this! Go, look at your list of names. Check to find those whom you haven't seen. Begin calling those on the list who told you to call back at a later time. Well, now it's later! Call them!

12
The Consultative Sales Process

Stage 3 – Getting the Appointment

This stage is exactly what it says it is. Get the appointment. Whether you are talking with the prospect in person or on the phone, the purpose of talking with them is to get the appointment. **It is not to discuss the oils**, dōTERRA®, wellness, or anything other than getting the appointment. Most of those with whom you share a close relationship won't even care what the reason is for getting together, they'll just need you to call and ask if they'd like to get together. These are people with whom you have a relationship. They are not strangers. They'll want to get with you.

Not long ago I was in a local Publix store and just as I was leaving I spotted a younger guy whom I hadn't seen in several years. I knew he'd gone through a divorce and had made a few career changes but nothing beyond that. As I began walking toward him, he caught my movement out of the corner of his eye and turning, exclaimed, "George! How are you doing?" After briefly catching up he asked me this question, "Hey, could we get together and talk?" I said sure and never thought to ask him what it was about. We had and have a relationship as friends. We don't always

> *The purpose of getting the appointment is to get the appointment*

have to tell people what we'll talk about or why we want to see them - just that we want to see them. If you are following what I'm advocating in this book about building relationships, becoming a leader, wanting to serve and love others, and helping people become what they were created to be, then most of the time your friends won't even ask what the purpose is for getting together. They'll just want to get together.

This might be a good time to briefly discuss using emails and texts for setting appointments with people. If the person with whom you are asking for an appointment is close enough to you that you can use either an email or text and/or because this is their preferred method of contact, then you can use either at your discretion. However, if you should use either of these methods, then again, the purpose of the email or text is to get the appointment. Don't try and "share" with them via this method of communication; it won't work.

If, when you're asking them for a time to visit and they ask what it's all about tell them in a few words that it's about an idea or concept that you're using to help keep you and/or your family healthier. Remember, the purpose of the phone call or personal chat is to get an appointment with them. This holds especially true for emails and texts.

In communicating with others, the best way is in person; the second best is a phone conversation or a Zoom or other web-based face-to-face over the internet; the third is an email; and the fourth is a text message. There is a progression of lost communication moving from the best way to number four. Communication is always prone to having a certain level of "noise" which distorts what we're trying to share and what others hear. Noise is interference with the intention of the communication of the sender and the comprehension of the receiver of the message s/he hears and understands. There are numerous factors to consider in understanding what can cause our communication with others to fail. The following are some of those causes: environmental noise, physiological-impairment noise, semantic noise, syntactical noise, organizational noise, cultural noise, and psychological noise. In other words, keep it simple and keep it on task that the purpose of asking for an appointment is just that, to get the appointment. This is as true in our primary communication as it is regarding our use of essential oils; less is more.

13
The Consultative Sales Process

Stage 4 – Initial Meeting/Assessing Needs

Now, when you get to the initial meeting place, this is where you can share with your friend what you've been doing. But the primary purpose of this meeting is to listen to what your friend is saying, gather facts about what s/he both thinks and feels about wellness, and determine if s/he is open to learning more about how to care for her/his health and her/his family's health. This is the fact-gathering time for you to not only hear the words but to also listen to what isn't being said. Seventy percent of all communication is non-verbal. Therefore, when you are with someone, listen to what they're doing as well as to what they're saying. Look at their behavior. Observe them. However, be careful here. There are a significant number of judging types of techniques that are promoted as ways to identify what a person is feeling or thinking. These types of techniques are less helpful than they are helpful unless you've been professionally trained in these techniques and are using them in a professional career. Generally, without this professional training they do more damage than good because you are judging the actions of a person without knowing the underlying values, thought processes, social style, or personality.

> *Listen to what people do more than what they say*

For example, when a person is sitting across from you with their arms folded, there are types of behavioral techniques that will tell you the person is closed or walled off and isn't interested. This may or may not be true. In fact, in most cases this is not a true conclusion. When we study nonverbal behavior we have to consider context, the environment, and all the behaviors we see, not just one. That means reading all of the body, from head to toe. Unfortunately, myths about nonverbal clues abound and arm crossing is one that is too often erroneously seen by the undiscerning as a blocking behavior when in fact there may be a variety of very different reasons for it. So, look for a conceptual flavor of the person as they are both speaking and listening.

Your greatest tool at this time is your questions. If you are more interested in the prospect than in what you have to say about the oils, wellness, dōTERRA®, or your experience with them, then you'll have pertinent questions because you'll be listening to the prospect. And what topic is most important to the prospect? You got it! They are! The prospect! They are their most favorite subject and because they are, by your centering your questions on them, they will respond.

Several years ago I was in my office, sitting at my desk, working on some possible solutions for one of the donors with whom I was working. One of our planned gift officers asked, as he was entering my office, if I had some time to discuss a potential donor with him. I kept an open-door policy and all of the team knew they could interrupt anything I was doing at any time. I told him I'd be glad to listen and see what I could offer. While still standing across the desk from me, the planned gift officer said he'd been having trouble getting one of his donors to open up and he was stymied as to how he could help the donor complete a gift. The officer believed the donor wanted to give a gift to the university and the donor had actually said so, but this is where the process had stalled. However, when I had joined the officer in a meeting with them, the donor and his wife opened up and shared things that this officer hadn't even considered talking about with them. He wanted to know how I did "it." I asked him what he meant by "it." He asked me how I get people to open up so easily with me and he asked me why he hadn't been able to get any information from them. I said that's easy. I am genuinely interested in each person I talk with. They have a story to tell. I like stories. By my being curious about who they are, how they got where they are in life, how they arrived at their thinking, etc. they are willing to talk about their favorite subject…themselves; and I was always honored they would tell me about such a great subject. The "prospect" always knew I am more interested in them and what their needs are than in anything else.

To better demonstrate to this young gift officer how this worked, I suggested we role play. He would be the gift officer and I'd be the potential donor. About five minutes into the role play, I could immediately see what was wrong. Paul, the gift officer, would ask a question, get an answer, move to another question, get an answer and so on; but he never connected and built on each preceding question. It was like being asked by your best friend about the latest movie you'd seen, but instead of being interested in the story of the movie and wondering what happened next, he moved from question to question with no bridging of how it all fit together. There was an obvious lack of connection and interest on the part of the officer to relate. It was as though he was filling in the blanks of a form with no personal interest in the data or the person the data represented. To the gift officer it was all demographic data and a means to get to the part where the donor gave a gift to the university. To me, they were telling me short stories of their lives which when connected provided me with a sense of who they were and are so I could meet them at their current juncture of life. So with this approach, I was not only introduced to them, I learned who they were, what made them tick, how they felt about their children, their parents, what inspired them, and more.

Unfortunately, the scenario that my planned gift officer faced is too true for so many people attempting to "sell" something or in getting people "to want to buy" something. When asking questions in this initial meeting of the process, take your time; be interested in them; listen to what they're saying and to what they are not saying; ask for clarification when you don't quite get what they are talking about; test yourself from time to time by re-stating what they said in your own words and at the same time ask them if what you just said is actually what they meant. Spend time here because this is the stage of the sales process which sets up what you'll say when it is time to close the sale. And remember an extremely important point that David Stirling shared at the 2014 dōTERRA® national convention. Remember? I told you earlier that he

> *"people are either in a crisis, have just come through a crisis, or about to enter a crisis…"*

said when you meet someone, understand they are probably in a crisis, have just come out of a crisis, or they are about to enter a crisis, and most of the time you'll be correct. Approach each meeting with a prospect with this kind of caring in mind.

14
The Consultative Sales Process

Stage 5 – Presentation of Solution(s)

We're now at stage 5. Do you remember Stage 1? Know your product by knowing what the features, the advantages, and the benefits of each product are. We're now at the point where knowing about the benefits lays the groundwork for the presentation. Presenting the solution(s) to the prospect is all about answering their questions and helping them solve their problem. It is not about us; it's about them. The facts which you gathered in Stage 4 should have uncovered and revealed to you and to the prospect what the prospect sees as a need. Here is where a combination of the products you offer and the concepts of how to apply your products to the prospect's needs are laid out in a presentation. Sometimes a presentation is more formal and presented in a written analysis with recommendations. However, most of the time in our working with our prospects, this will be a verbal presentation, and nothing will be written. Sometimes this is referred to as part of a Wellness Consult where a questionnaire was filled out and a verbal discussion/presentation is used to present recommendations to the prospect. If this is the case, then the concepts discussed in Stage 4 of this process should be applied when filling out the form and the concepts in Stage 5 should be applied when making the recommendations.

> *Success in Stage 5 is based on how well you've learned and applied Stage 1*

Either way is a good and acceptable format. A combination of both verbal and written may be better suited for some of your prospects. But, whatever and however you make a presentation to the prospect, this is the stage in the consultative sales process where the whole meeting is about the prospect. Stage 5 of the Consultative Sales process is successful for you and the prospect because of your knowledge and application of the benefits of the concepts of wellness, the essential oil products, and dōTERRA® as a provider of the products as you apply all these to the solutions you offer the prospect.

By your knowing the advantages and benefits of wellness, essential oils, and dōTERRA® as discussed in Stage 1, you'll be able to connect one or more solutions to your prospect's needs, thereby providing you with the information and concepts of making a presentation. You're connecting the dots for them to travel from where they are in their wellness life to where they want to be, and you get the privilege of helping them get there. This stage of the sales process is generally what we get to hear from others whether it be in front of an audience of many or an audience of one. We'll give standing ovations to those who tell their stories and who chose to transform their lives and/or the lives of their families because someone helped them connect the dots and showed them a solution to their situation.

Keep the following in mind when you are beginning to build your team and business. You don't have to be the guru of all gurus on all things dōTERRA®, essential oils, or the concept of multiplication, etc., yet. You have a sponsor tree of people who can and want to help you make your first few presentations. Just ask...They'll help!

Regardless of the help you receive from your team, strategically use individual meetings with others. Remember that you can impress others from a stage, but you will impact them when you engage them individually.

15
The Consultative Sales Process

Stage 6 – The Close

The first time I was interviewed for the position as the Director of Planned Giving at Auburn University, the process took an entire afternoon and consisted of three separate meetings. My first meeting was with the Vice President for Development and it consisted of the two of us talking for about 40 minutes. He then escorted me to a room where there were five others seated, waiting for my arrival.

This meeting lasted for about an hour with them asking me lots of questions about planned gifts, my background in planned giving, how I worked with donors, and how I worked with co-workers, etc. After they'd finished their questioning, they asked me if I had any questions. I said I did. I looked at the Assistant Vice President for Development and asked, "Why are you interested in me?" He looked at me and quizzically said, "I'm not sure what you mean." I replied, "Why are you interested in me? I don't have the traditional pedigree (I used this word on purpose to see if there was any humor in any of them; there wasn't) of having come up through the ranks of administration before entering planned giving. So, why me and what are you looking for?"

I loved his reply. He said, "Our biggest problem in raising money for Auburn is that we don't have anyone who knows how to close. We have lots of people who are interested in giving a gift to Auburn, but we don't have people who know how to motivate the donor to complete the transaction." I don't think they expected my reaction. I laughed. Not at them. But I laughed. I was laughing because I knew something they didn't. Their development officers had done all of the work necessary to complete the giving of a gift but had left out the simplest and easiest stage of the sales process. The Close. I knew that 95% of the entire sales process was done prior to the close. The close consists of about 5% of the work, yet people always seem to blame the lack of a sale on the close.

> *The close is only 5% of the sales process*

I explained that the close is the easiest part of the process and that I could easily close cases. They did look at me like I'd just landed from Mars, but they must have believed me because they left and the next round of interviewers came in; all 27 of them…I counted. These were the majority of people in all the departments I'd be working with and they were being given an opportunity to meet me and ask questions. You know what their most significant question was? Did I know how to close? When I answered this time, I was more judicious, and I attempted less comedy in my answer. I shared with them that, indeed, I do know how to close and I find that closing the sale is the easiest part of the whole process.

So, how do you close? You ask. You ask the prospect if the benefits you showed them make sense to them and if the benefits meet the need for their solution. If their answer is yes, then you ask them the correct spelling of their name, their mailing and billing address and which credit card they wish to use. You simply ask!

Once you've asked them to make this decision, that's it; you've closed. There are three answers the prospect will give you:

- They will want to become a Wellness Advocate or a Wholesale Customer immediately by working with you to fill out the form and provide you with all necessary information for its completion whether on line or on paper.
- They will want some time to think about this. This could mean they need some more time to think about the decision, they may need to check with their spouse due to budgetary constraints, they may not be interested enough about caring for their own wellness but they're intrigued with a particular oil or product, or any number of other reasons. The key point in this is that if they say they need more time, this is not the same as saying no. Give them enough time, but be sure to get back with them and follow up asking them about their decision.
- They may say no; they're not interested. Sometimes that means no. Sometimes that means now yet.

Regardless of the answer, what you've done is made the ask and you've closed. The response is up to them. This is an important part of this stage because you need to know that you have asked and that you haven't simply shared about the oils and hoped they might ask you if they could buy.

When I was on the staff of a Christian organization, I shared how college students could come to know Jesus and have a relationship with Him. In my first year with the organization I shared with a freshman how he could know Christ and have that personal relationship with Him. At the end of my first meeting with the student, I asked him if he'd like to ask Christ into his life. His response was - not at that time. I assured him it was ok and went on to explain that at some point in his life he might want to have this personal relationship with Jesus. He said that he might be interested in the future.

My next question to him was, "If you should decide to ask Jesus into your life, in the future, would you know how?" He said he wasn't sure, so I asked his permission to explain how he could do this in the future. He said that'd be ok. I went over the explanation of prayer, that it is talking with God, that God knows our hearts and isn't as concerned with our words, and that if the prayer at the back of the booklet I had shared expressed the desire of this young man's heart, he could either use these words to talk with God or he could use his own words which would express his desire to ask Jesus into his heart. He then shared with me that if he ever wanted to ask Jesus into his heart, he'd know how.

About a year later I was walking down the steps of the student union on that college campus, heading home for the day. A young guy passed me, turned and said, "George, hey George, remember me?" Unfortunately, I didn't. He quickly reminded me of who he was and our last conversation together. He said that he still hadn't asked Jesus into his life, but he knew how when and if he ever became interested. He said there were too many things he wanted to experience as a student before he would be ready to quit having fun, (his words, not mine). He went on and said he'd heard our organization had been trying to get into his fraternity to share about Jesus for several years and that his fraternity had always said no. He had become the social chairman of the fraternity and it was part of his responsibility to determine who would be allowed to make presentations to the guys in the frat. He concluded by telling me that if I ever wanted to get in to speak to the guys, he'd be glad to arrange it because he remembered how I treated him and never pushed anything on him. I said I'd like that and asked when I could arrange a time to come speak with them, which I did.

Even though the people we share with regarding wellness and the oils may not be ready today or may not even be interested today doesn't mean they won't be in the future. When we ask people to make a decision, we are giving closure to both them and us as far as a decision that is needing to be made; but that decision doesn't have to be in the affirmative today. The second most important part of the close after the ask is that there is a clear understanding to the prospect that they know how they can purchase the oils at a wholesale price and continue getting them. Think about this as an educational process that will be ongoing.

But, during the close, they need to know two things: there needs to be a **decision** made on purchasing the oils and they need to **know how** they can purchase the oils when they're ready if they decide not to purchase right then. There is a third element here that should be introduced and you should consider as important. If a person is still someone with whom you want to work, be sure to tell them that we work in teams and that you'd really like them to be on your team. Be sure they know how to contact you if and when they are ready to join. And, be sure they know that they matter to you! Always leave people better in some way than when you found them.

Here are some sample closing statements:

- "Do you believe this solution (these oils) will meet your needs?

- "So, just to recap, you really like the oils, what they can do to help you and your family, and that they are natural. So, let's go ahead and process that order for you, OK?"

- "Is there anything that would prevent you from getting started with the oils today?" If the answer is no, begin filling out the form.

- "I would like to work with you for your wellness and/or for the wellness of your family. I'd like you to be on my team! Are you ready now?"

Regardless of what "closing statement" you use, the point of the close is to ask! As you get more practice in closing, you'll find that the close is a natural progression from the previous five stages. Therefore, in a short time span you'll adapt your own and/or adopt from the suggestions, words you feel comfortable using and you'll make them your own. But never forget, closing the sale is very simple; ASK.

16
The Consultative Sales Process

Stage 7 – Follow Up or Teammate Education

You've studied the oils to learn about their features, advantages, and benefits; you've identified those people with whom you'd like to work; you've asked these people for an appointment; you've learned about what they are interested in; you've presented a solution to their situation; and you've asked them to buy the oils. You should be done, right? Wrong! This seventh stage is where the work begins. This is all about maintaining and building on your relationship with them.

If they've said no

If the prospect you've asked to join says, "no," you need to consider this as only the beginning. Studies show that it takes an average of **six to eight contacts** with a prospect before they will either confirm their initial decision of "no" or they decide to join. Most people stop at **two contacts**; the initial contact through a phone call, email, or text and a second contact where either the person joins or says, "no." Most Wellness Advocates

> *Studies show that a person needs 6-8 contacts for a decision…most people stop at 2-3 or even 1*

looking to add people to their team never get past the initial contact either on the phone or in person. You need to keep track of your prospects, especially those who are your friends prior to your involvement in wellness and the oils.

If they need more information

If they say they need more information, find out, by asking them, how they would prefer to receive the information they're requesting. Understanding how a person prefers to be treated speaks directly to how they prefer to receive information from you. Knowing which behavioral style is their preferred style is a great start. However they prefer to receive the information, tell them you'll get it for them in "x" amount of time and then make good on what you said you'd do by doing it. This will show them you are serious about helping others, they are important to you, their request is important to you, and that you are working as a professional. Never leave this hanging! For every time the prospect wants information you must have control of the situation (not the person) by getting the information to them within the agreed upon time frame and then discussing with them a time you'll either call or meet them to discuss what they've studied and researched. This is not being pushy. This is recognizing there is a large body of information to learn about the oils and wellness and it is impossible for a person on their own to grasp important aspects of the information you've provided them. Be courteous, kind, and professional by getting back to them and not leaving them hanging. This is a business. Treat it like one!

If they say yes

This is where your work and their growth into wellness and the oils begins:

- multiplication
- oil education
- helping them identify what it is they wish to have happen from their use of the oils; their goals

If they've decided to become a builder, they need to learn about running a business. This stage is the seventh of the process, but it is the first stage of mentoring and coaching them to their success regardless of whether they are using the oils, sharing the oils, or wanting to build a business with the oils.

Whatever the answer from the prospect, you are going to need some way to manage keeping track of whom you are doing what with. This is called Contact Relationship Management. You can keep track of what you're doing with prospects and teammates on paper or through electronic means. On paper, this has to be more than writing their names in a notebook. You'll need at a minimum a calendar for an entire year with enough space to write their names and what the next step is with each of them. If you want to use an electronic means of keeping track of people, there are some no or low-cost tools to help you do this. Microsoft Outlook is one of those free tools. Talk to your upline and keep going upline until you find someone with a method that you feel comfortable using and then use it.

One final word on this stage. Regardless of the decision the prospect makes, the effect you'll have on them and in their lives, is directly proportional to this:

You can impress people from a distance, but you'll only impact them up close.

17

Conclusion

More Like Me

Hopefully, throughout this book you've been catching glimpses of how unique you and everyone you meet are. Though this is true, I am saddened by the continued use of tools and methods which teach and train people to be just like everyone else. And lately, I've seen a number of people who, though they have gone through training in the area of strengths and are now certified to call themselves coaches, have little understanding of the tools they employ. Though the training to better understand and apply their and others' strengths promotes the value of expanding on a person's strengths, some of these coaches manipulate the assessment tool in order to change the ranking in order of their own strength themes. Yeah, you read this correctly! I've watched a Facebook video of a person who advertised herself as a trained and certified coach as she explained why she repeatedly re-took the Strengths Assessment because she felt others were taking advantage of a Strength Theme which ranked as number one of her Top 5 Strengths. She wanted to rid herself of this Strength Theme as being in her Top 5 and she was proud that by her repeated re-taking of the Assessment, she drove that particular Strength Theme to be reported as a number 15 in her list position.

Changing your Strength Theme by retesting because you don't like a theme or you think it isn't what you consider to be as valuable as another strength theme is similar to the farmer who continues to check the weight of the same pig hoping to change the breed of the pig. Manipulative coaches fail to understand that it's not the testing and re-testing of their strengths in order to change their strength themes which provides the difference, but it's identifying and applying the natural ones that each person is born with that provides the difference. Our talents are what we're given at birth. The strength themes are the organizing of our talents and strengths in order to better identify what and possibly how our talents and strengths might be used; and I stress, *might be used*. You see, it's up to each of us, as unique individuals, to determine how we choose to use our talents.

That coach's retesting of herself is a gross misuse and misunderstanding of the value of that particular coach's talents and strengths. This is, in my opinion, coaching negligence in her practice relative to the value of her talents and strengths.

> *"You must be careful how you walk and where you go for there are those following who will set their feet where you set yours."*
> Robert E. Lee

And, this is a travesty to the people whom she coaches, their lives, and their growth in their knowledge, application of talents and strengths, and strategic use as they seek to work out their success and their serving of others through their natural gifts and strengths. Any person aspiring to be a coach should always be very careful as to what they teach because as a coach they will be held to a higher standard.

What is this higher standard? A coach instructs others on how to lay and build a foundation to improve their lives. If what is taught is not solid, strong, and able to withstand difficulties, then the coach shall be judged as having destroyed the opportunities that could have been enjoyed.

Without a strong foundation in building construction, it is true that the integrity of the entire building is questionable. This is just as true in our lives. It is our responsibility to build our lives upon a rock-solid foundation, so we can enjoy life, endure hardships, and succeed in our vision. So, be careful who you follow and what they are teaching.

> *"Let not many of you become teachers (coaches), my brethren, knowing that as such we will incur a stricter judgment."*
> James 3:1 The Bible (NASB)

Be assured that you were designed and created for a purpose - a purpose only you can achieve due to your unique behavioral style and your talents plus other inherent and acquired attributes. You were not designed and engineered for success by listening to, believing in, and then attempting to be like someone else or by the re-assessing of your strength themes to manipulate results. A good coach will assist you in becoming your best self by building on the foundation of your life given to you at birth – your own unique style and strengths.

Throughout our lives we encounter various situations and circumstances. It is the application of our talents which are developed into strengths that brings out the special and unique person we were created to be. We become the spice of life for the benefit of and in the lives of others. And, we benefit by knowing that it is through us, our unique talent set, that we are able to serve others. The results of our proper use of our gifts benefits others and ourselves. We feel fulfilled. We feel energized. We became a hero in the life or lives of others for a moment. No fanfare necessary. No publicity needed. Knowing that our talents, our strengths used for the benefit of another person matters, that our own life matters, and that we make a difference, is a significant, key element in our knowing our "why," our purpose, for being alive at this moment in time. In all the possibilities of times and epochs when we could have been born and have grown into adulthood, this is the time for which we were created with our specific talents and our specific style of behavior. This is your time…

A Whole Lot More Like Me

I get asked by a lot of people why it is that they can get along well with some people and with others, not so much. I love this question, especially when it's from a husband and wife. For most of my 30+ years of teaching and training on behavioral styles through the SOCIAL STYLE MODEL™®, I was doing this in a business setting. So, when I began to open up this material to people outside of their work environment, I was excited and amazed to see how positive the impact is on couples. I always knew the value of this behavioral model, but I had never seen and heard first-hand the depth to which it is of value in clarifying roles and in some cases saving marriages.

Too often in my working with and getting closer to people, I've learned that one of the spouses in the marriage has been withdrawing from the relationship. What I've found is that in order to relieve the tension that builds up due to normal, everyday marital situations, one person has suppressed their style of behavior to appease a spouse and hopefully to lessen tension and even possibly save the marriage. However, this often leads to further tension and eventual crisis situations which can end in divorce anyway. Sometimes, and most often, it leads to one and eventually both partners living in quiet desperation and in surrendered relational vitality. So, instead of a dynamic and growing relationship, instead of a love relationship, it becomes a "he does his thing, she does her thing" coexistence. Spouses lose sight of who and what made each so interesting and exciting to the other to be with when the relationship and marriage first began. They've lost their interest in and ability to grow into the, "whole lot more like me" life they were meant to experience.

*We are **born** with our behavioral style*

Now, here comes the good part. When individuals and couples have attended my seminars and they've been engaged in learning about social behavioral styles, their own particular style, and the preferred style of their significant other, there is often a feeling almost like being handed a free "get out of jail card." There is a feeling of relief in knowing their own style of behavior, though sometimes frowned on by others, is still a legitimate style. They learn that it is ok for them to be exactly like themselves. They learn that by their working so hard to please others, they have become less like themselves and more like someone they haven't wanted to become, haven't intended to become, or in some cases, someone they don't even like.

> *We are **born** with our unique talents from which, through practice, we develop strengths.*

They have a feeling of having lost themselves...lost who they are. Then, when they've learned that their behavioral style is what they were born with, what God gave them at birth for a purpose, they can begin to relax and to realize their value personally and in the lives of others.

Granted, they can't just go rushing out and exert their style of behavior on others and think it's acceptable to do so. Part of the education and training through this tool is to not only learn about the ability to accept their own style of behavior, but also to allow others the freedom to express their own behavioral style as well. This is called Versatility. And the learning and practice of Versatility is the crux, the pivotal element, for success in building relationships. Additionally, it has the same crucial value when we learn about our talents and strengths. The ability to not lose ourselves and at the same time

> ***Versatility** is the ability to be comfortable in your behavioral style while adjusting to the behavioral style of others*

not force others to behave and work out their talents in the same manner as we must is really freedom. Yes, freedom! Freedom to let me be "a whole lot more like I am" and the freedom to let others be a whole lot more like the self they were created to be!

One last thought before I leave the talents and behavioral style sections. I have heard many people tell me and others they could tell another person's Strength Themes after observing them for a short while. Unfortunately, too often I've had people do this after a couple of minutes of observation. I assert here: It is not possible to observe a person for a few minutes and accurately determine what Strength Theme or Themes they have. Not only is it not possible, but it is contrary to Dr. Donald Clifton's teaching.

Prior to the CliftonStrengths® Assessment, all we had to go on was observation. We could observe a person's seemingly effortless ability to perform a task. But, we knew that our observing the person perform one task was not sufficient. We needed to observe them over a period of time performing similar and dissimilar tasks in order to get a better read on what they might have for talents or strengths. When we attempt to place a person into a Strength Theme through a quick few minutes of observation, what we're really doing is placing them in a tidy box. It may not be our intention, but in effect it is what we are doing. We're pigeon-holing a person by our surmised expertise in what a person has for a Strength Theme. I don't know about you, but whenever someone has attempted to pigeon-hole me, they've made an assumption about me that is more often wrong than right. How about you? Ever had that happen to you? I didn't like it. Did you? The point of knowing our own and others' Strength Themes is not for pigeon-holing at all.

The point is for us to expand on our talents, to strategically use our talents, and to complement each other by building on each other's talents in many and varied situations. Also, when we compliment someone on our team we can do so by knowing specific talents they've used. We can provide them with a specific rather than the general pat on the back.

Keep in mind, the value of the CliftonStrengths Assessment is that it gives all of us a commonality of words and language so that we are better able to communicate and to serve others. It is faulty reasoning for us to shoot from the hip with our snap judgments of another's Strength Theme.

The value of knowing another person's Strength Theme doesn't lie in knowing the Strength Theme. The value lies in knowing the talents and strengths which make up that person's Strength Theme. And this brings up my final point in this discussion at this time. Too many people are using the General Description of a Strength Theme as the basis for giving advice on a person's talents and strengths. In the Clifton Strengths Assessment model, the General Theme Description is a great tool to help us better understand the broad growth capabilities of a particular Strength Theme; however that description is not specific to any one person, it is a generalization of what the Strength Theme has the capability of expanding into.

Let me say this again! In the Clifton Strengths Assessment model, the General Theme Description is a great tool to better understand the broad capabilities of a particular Strength Theme, however it is not specific to any one person. To see and then gain some insight into an individual's talents, we need to be using the right tool. The Strengths Insight Report is the correct report. Only inside of this report do we get to look behind the curtain and see the talents of an individual. After all, it's the talents that we were born with, not the Strength Theme. And it's the compilation of varied talents that build the Strength Theme in each individual that counts. In depth study of talents will show that talent groupings form individual strengths. As an example, one person's Strengths might include a number of talents that are exactly the same as someone who has those talents included in a different Strength Theme.

Comfort Zone

I know that I only briefly touched on my conviction that in general, there has been a misuse of the phrase, "comfort zone." This phrase has become a catchall of blame for everything that keeps us from achieving our full potential. From motivational speakers to the study of psychology, we are constantly bombarded to get out of our "anxiety-neutral" condition in order to be more and do more. We're told that our "comfort zone" is a place where we have little or no stress and that some tension or stress is good for us in order to achieve goals and objectives. On the concept of having some tension to achieve goals and objectives, I do agree. Yet, what we are more accurately being told, I believe, is that we are to get out of our "complacent zone."

Think about this. All the times you've been told to get out of your "comfort zone" how did you feel and what were your thoughts on this? An educated guess based on my discussions with others is that we normally assumed that something is wrong with us and that in order for us to become successful we must change ourselves to be like someone else. It didn't just cause some tension, it sent shockwaves through our system. It didn't uplift us, it denigrated us. It caused us to think less of ourselves. We were being told that up until that point in our lives, we were some degree of failure. For most people it causes them to shut down on their own capabilities and question how they could have been so wrong for so long about themselves.

Actually, there's something about the phrase "comfort zone" that has a sense of familiarity and ease in our life. It makes us feel, well, comfortable. And face it, in this hectic, fast-paced and impersonal world, don't all of us want a little more comfort in our lives?

It's interesting that this is exactly how the Merriam-Webster dictionary defines comfort zone - "the level at which one functions with ease and familiarity." And, let's not forget, when we use the phrase "comfort zone" in describing or explaining an aspect or something about our life, shouldn't we feel and even think a little better about ourselves when we are in that zone? I believe there is a reason for this. I believe we were created to live smack dab in the middle and fullness of our "comfort zones." And I believe that most people don't take the challenge to live in their "comfort zone." I believe they live in a complacent zone, or they're striving to live up a phantom image of who they should be, or they're in the process of throwing away who they were created to be in order to become like someone else.

It fits, too, with the Merriam-Webster definition that our comfort zone, where we function with ease and familiarity, is similar to our proper use of our talents and strengths. When we are using our talents and strengths we are producing a near perfect performance for those tasks for which we are suited. It is in our comfort zone where we find who we were created to be. Our comfort zone is where we do our best work. Our comfort zone is where our individual behavioral style and talents reside. Our comfort zone is where we should reside. I believe we need to quit trying to get out of our comfort zone and for the first time in our lives work at getting the most out of ourselves within our comfort zone. As I said, I believe most people live outside of their comfort zone. Just don't confuse the phrase that is currently used about living in our comfort zone with what is our actually living in a complacent zone.

> *It takes hard work to break into our* **Comfort Zone** *by knowing and applying our behavioral style and our talents!*

I believe it is hard to get into our real comfort zone in the negative world in which we live. Breaking out of the negative ideas and feelings we have told ourselves and/or others have said to or about us and moving toward our designed value takes work. By identifying, realizing, accepting, and then believing in our own value, we can rise up to living in our comfort zone. To achieve this takes hard work, strategic thinking and planning, diligence in knowing ourselves, and a resolve to never give up on who we were created to be. We were endowed with our behavioral style, we were engineered with our talents, and every one of us was instilled with a vision of our being great in the areas where our talents naturally take us. Focus on this and you will not only "feel a whole lot more like you do right now" but you will be a whole lot more like you were created to be! And there is nothing like that feeling!

And now for the final word. The title of this book comes from one of Norma's uncles; Curtis Dominey. Uncle Curtis was known for his home spun humor, intellect, wisdom, and all round infectious sayings. For those of us who had the privilege of knowing him, he was one of LA's (Lower Alabama) kindest, gentlest, wisest, most humorous, and loving Tom Sawyer-esque gentlemen anyone ever met. So it is from one of his sayings that the title of this book evolved.

"I feel a whole lot more like I do right now, than I did a while ago!"

May all of us experience the wisdom of Uncle Curtis each and every day of our lives. And may each thrive using your SOCIAL STYLE® with your talents and strengths, right smack -dab in the middle of your very own, very productive, and very successful comfort zone. You may sweat like crazy learning, developing your talents, and strategically applying them. But in the end, it's worth it to feel a whole lot more like your authentic you. Then you can really love YOUR comfort zone.

ABOUT THE AUTHOR

George E. Willock has been in the charitable planning field for the past 25 years. He started a charitable consulting firm, then continued his career working with Auburn University as the Director of Trusts, Estates, and Gift Planning. During his 14 years at Auburn University, he and his team raised over $650 million in planned gifts with $103 million of those gifts coming from a nationally acclaimed charitable life insurance model which he created. In 2014, George left Auburn University, co-founding WWLC, LLC.

Prior to George's work in the charitable planning field, he spent 15 years in the estate and financial planning field working in sales, agent training, and management. While there he learned, modified, and excelled in consultative selling to better serve his clients.

George has completed his Chartered Life Underwriter (CLU®) designation, the Life Underwriter Training Council Fellowship (LUTCF®) designation, is a graduate of the National Planned Giving Institute (NPGI®), completed the Chartered Advisor in Philanthropy (CAP®) designation, earned the Accredited Estate Planner's (AEP®) designation, and is a TRACOM Certified SOCIAL STYLE MODEL™® & Versatility Instructor. His articles have appeared in several publications and he has authored coursework for The American College of Financial Services in Bryn Mawr, Pennsylvania.

George speaks regionally and nationally on Planned Giving including Charitable Life Insurance and Building Successful Interpersonal Relationships with SOCIAL STYLES®. Currently, through WWLC, LLC., George works as a consultant to charitable organizations and offers seminars on the use of the SOCIAL STYLE MODEL™® to improve relationships integrating the CliftonStrengths® Assessment.

Made in the USA
Columbia, SC
14 June 2019